Left at Hiva Oa

Eric'
Thank you for your
friendship & support!
For wars & future, also
in your adventure!")
Aloha
5/31/18

LEFT

AT

HIVA OA

A Novel

MALIA BOHLIN

The Library of Congress has cataloged this edition as follows:

Bohlin, Malia.
Left at Hiva Oa / Malia Bohlin

ISBN: 978-0-9993010-0-5

Dedicated to my mother, Jennifer.

Lele ka 'iwa, malie kai ko'o

"When the *'iwa* [frigate bird] flies,
the rough sea will be calm."

LEFT

AT

HIVA OA

PART I

CHAPTER ONE

March 14, 1962
Location: 5° 26' 30" S
                 115° 14' 52" W

"Man overboard!"

Leahy's voice carried over me in a gust as I climbed through the companionway and came on deck. He was alone at the helm. My eyes swept forward to the bow; indeed, there was no one on board but the two of us. I looked aft, scanning the deep blue water behind the boat. Twelve-foot swells rose and fell around us. Whiffs of spray blew off the tops of the waves, misting the air and clouding my view.

My eye caught something in the next wave. It was Patty, bobbing astern, her long blond hair afloat around her head. Up she went in a wall of water rising above us; down she disappeared on the other side. The life preserver followed her, a useless blur of white.

"Captain Ken?" William Leahy's ready brown eyes were on me, his hand on the tiller, waiting for direction.

"Bear away and prepare to tack back!" The practice from hundreds of man-overboard drills made my command automatic, even if I had never experienced a real emergency like this. One thing was sharp in my mind: a member of our crew was overboard and, as captain, I was responsible for her safety. I moved to the mast and looked back over the water as the *Gracias* slowly began to turn. Patty rose again, further now, at the top of the next crest, a valley of deep blue water between us.

At the mainmast I unhitched the line from around the cleat and dropped the sail. It fell into a crumpled pile, like sheets kicked to the bottom of a bed. I hastily wrapped a single tie around the sail and boom to keep them together. Using just the remaining foresail we would have to sail into the wind, tacking in a zigzag fashion to make our way back toward Patty. Time was of the essence. She would weaken quickly in these rough seas. There were also the dangers of being pushed under by a wave, going into hypothermic shock, and, of course, sharks. With a quick step, I jumped to the forward boom to unlock the winch.

We were fifteen days out of the Galapagos Islands on my forty-foot schooner, the *Gracias*. There we had enjoyed sunny days of diving and exploring. We found turtles too numerous to count, birds with blue feet, and many more of Darwin's wonderments. The diving was spectacular; I collected several beautiful shells to send home to my mother. We had a new, exotic fish for dinner each night. And lobster for lunch, if we felt like it. At the end of each day we convened on deck and marveled at the changing sky and falling sun as it sank in mere moments here at the equator.

Our third morning at anchor, Leahy came on deck wearing an old cowboy hat. The once-white crown was darkened with ages of dirt and the broad rim was trimmed with layers of murky fingerprints. Dark stubble covered his brown face and his eyes were red with last night's drink. He was the spitting image of a star in a Western movie; the once bright, idealistic young sheriff now battered, worn, and turned desperate outlaw.

"Howdy, pardner!"

"Where's the holdup?" I teased.

"You didn't have these at the Academy, did you, Captain Ken? I knew this old thing would come in handy. Kept my head cool on the plains of Colorado." He grinned and for emphasis pushed the hat down firmly with a flat palm on top of his head. "Ought to work here too."

"Don't let that thing blow overboard," I warned.

"Wouldn't dream of it." Leahy winked in my direction.

Patty appeared in her usual outfit of a bathing suit top and cutoff shorts. Her hair was wrapped under a scarf and large, glamorous sunglasses worthy of a movie star covered half of her small round face. She looked the part as she gave Leahy her broad beauty contestant's smile.

"Howdy, cowboy!"

"Howdy, ma'am!" He tipped his hat toward her.

With that showy display we set off to explore the low hills along this coastline.

We hiked inland, making our way slowly across old lava flows. They were black, rough, and blank; no trails were left behind on the hard, rocky surface. As we climbed higher, we discovered cool dark caves where we were greeted by strange pairs of red eyes and the soft flap of bat wings. Further up, we went through a forested area and found a freshwater stream. It bubbled by, clean, clear, and sparkling in the bits of sunlight that came through the treetops. It looked refreshing after so many days of bathing at sea. We jumped in. We swam, ate lunch, and swam again.

Leahy pulled out a flask of that rot-gut moonshine he'd bought from a farmer at the marina. He offered some my way, but I declined. Patty had a deep swig, and took another on my behalf. They could keep that among themselves; it was a hangover in a bottle, as far as I was concerned.

Late in the afternoon, we headed back toward the *Gracias*, picking our way between boulders and stepping carefully on the pebbly ground. Iguanas scampered ahead of us, leaving bursts of dust behind. Leahy squatted down onto the dry earth and watched them. With a sharp flick, he tossed his hat over one, trapping the creature. He came alongside and slowly lifted the edge of the hat, bent with his head near the ground. His narrow eyes squinted smaller in the bright sun.

"Yep, I got it. He's a pistol. Take a look."

Patty crept closer. She bent her small body next to him, wobbling slightly, her long hair swinging down to touch the ground. She pushed her sunglasses onto the top of her head, her eyes keen on seeing this creature. As Leahy peeled the edge of the hat off the red earth she jumped back with a screech.

"It tried to bite me!"

Leahy chuckled and let the hat down. "You think so?"

"I saw his tongue!"

I wanted to see for myself. Peering into the dark cave under the hat I spied the little iguana. Only six inches long, it must have been a youngster. He was backed up as far as he could get, facing me with the rest of his body curled along the inner rim of the hat. His tongue came out in a quick flash.

"I wonder how he'd like a life at sea?" I said.

"We'd have to keep a stash of flies for him," Leahy said. "Or do you think he could learn to eat fish?"

"Ew!!! No!! You fellows can't be serious." Patty's lips pouted and her forehead furrowed.

"Sure, every ship needs a mascot," I said. "They're good luck. Your dad must have had one."

She shrugged one shoulder and looked at Leahy.

"We should keep him," Leahy teased. "An iguana would make a terrific mascot."

She couldn't tell if we were pulling her leg or not.

The tales Patty told me when we met in Panama were unraveling like an old piece of line; split and frayed in a dozen directions. In our six weeks together I had seen none of the wisdom or practicality of the captain's daughter she claimed to be and only an abundant desire for adventure. She said she grew up sailing on her father's yacht in California; he taught her everything there was to know about the sea. But once onboard the *Gracias* she carelessly tied off the wrong knots and couldn't name a star above. And that incident with the beans! It turned out she was only nineteen. She was like a teenager who had snuck out after curfew on an escapade around the world.

Now, after Leahy's teasing, she came back with her charming smile. "Well, OK, but maybe we could get something cute, like a puppy?"

"A puppy would be great. But I haven't seen any around here." Leahy scooped up his hat. "You're free to go about your business, buddy. Stay out of trouble." The iguana took off, disappearing in a dark corner of stones.

We started back down the rocky slope. The ocean lay out before us, deep blue and sparkling in the afternoon sun. I could see the *Gracias* peacefully bobbing at her mooring in the bay. I felt proud seeing her there, quietly awaiting our return. She was both our home and our means of travel. She and I had already been a long way together, and years of voyaging still lay ahead.

Patty skipped in front of me. "Let's look for that puppy!"

"You know what I think?" I said to Leahy, as she moved down the hill ahead of us.

"What?"

"I think when God was handing out brains, Patty thought He said trains." Leahy looked at me sideways, waiting for what came next. "And she asked for a slow one!"

He laughed a big belly laugh. "Lucky for her, when He was handing out looks, she thought He said 'books' and asked for some good ones!" He was right, it was the best thing she had going for her.

Now, this silly girl was adrift. I shook my head in disbelief, in resigned disappointment. I'd made a stupid, deadly mistake.

The day started fair enough; around noon the wind picked up, as did the waves. Now, an hour later, the seas were churning, and we were dipping and rising in hard seas. By my reckoning this morning, the Marquesas were at least another 1,500 miles away. In fifteen days since leaving the Galapagos we had passed no other ships, had seen no one but ourselves. The three of us were alone on the high seas.

I didn't fear the ocean. The last few years with her had made us friends. Her salt seemed to have left a permanent layer on my round, tanned face and sun-blond hair; my protruding ears seemed to stand out just to better hear her every slap against the hull. Her rhythms were embedded in my long legs and I easily sprung about the deck barefoot, the wind on my bare chest. I knew her moods and her whims. Fun and willing some days, feisty and impervious on others. She may show a different face from day to day but her character never wavered; she would always be true to herself first, above all else.

"Don't ever take it personally," Lieutenant Rainy, our sailing coach at the Academy, once told me. "She is who she is and that's all she'll ever be. Sooner you learn that, the sooner you two will be in accord." He chuckled. "You might want to remember that if you ever find a wife," he added, almost to himself.

Now it was time to work with this wild mood of hers that pitched the *Gracias* forward and back and had knocked one of our crew into her swells.

Following my directions, Leahy stayed at the helm while I cranked the winch. The long, sturdy boom that supported the bottom of the foresail swung across the deck, aligning the sail in the opposite direction. The *Gracias* turned and pitched heavily to the left, and suddenly we were heeling deeply with just twelve inches between the water and the edge of the port deck. Pitching up and down in the twelve-foot swells, we headed back toward where we had come from. Patty was starboard, to the right; as we got closer, we prepared to switch the sail again.

"Ready?" I called through the wind to Leahy.

"Ready!"

I unlocked the winch and cranked it back. The sail moved over and the *Gracias* roughly pitched starboard, headed toward Patty. We were careful to give her a wide berth, lest the current push us into her. We got within ten yards, rising and falling together in the swells.

Leahy secured a quick bowline knot at the bitter end of a hundred-foot nylon rope and, like the world's most desperate cowboy, gave it a swing above his strong, lithe body and a fierce launch in Patty's direction.

The *Gracias* went down between crests and we watched the rope land above us on the next wave. A wall of water between us, we saw nothing of Patty. Then, as we rose on the next crest, we saw her rise as well. She spotted the line and launched from some supernatural point in the water, diving off the wave carrying her and into the trough where the rope lay, landing on top of it. She grasped the loop and as she rose again up the next crest, Leahy pulled her toward us, hand over hand on the thick white rope.

I took the helm and adjusted the *Gracias* to the swells, heaving to a forty-five-degree angle against the waves to ride up them smoothly and ease the downward impact. As Leahy pulled Patty abreast of the boat, she rose with the water beside us. He reached down to lift her aboard.

She flopped on the deck onto her side, blond hair flung about, naked as the day she was born. A pool of seawater formed around her on the white fiberglass deck. Her bare feet trembled, white and wrinkled. She lay in a loose pile, her back heaving as she fought to catch her breath. Pushing herself up into a sitting position, she sputtered and coughed as she searched for air. She was a soggy mess. Her hair was twisted and stringy and her lips were blue from the cold. From behind her blond tangle of locks she looked up at Leahy standing next to her.

"You saved me!" she gasped out. Her blue eyes were bright with zeal and she suddenly smiled wide. Her arms reached skyward toward Leahy as if for an embrace.

"Nothing anyone wouldn't do for their crew." Leahy put a hand toward her to help her up.

"You're my hero, Billy." She struggled to get her balance in the surge, then finally stood and hugged him wholeheartedly, every naked, soaked inch of her pressed against him. They swayed together with the rough pitch of the boat.

He peeled her arms from around his neck and stepped between us to pick up her towel, tucked under the lid of the rear hatch. She took it and quickly wrapped it around herself.

He glanced at me. "Well, Patty, it was a team effort. Captain helped too." He looked back at her face. "You sure gave me a scare. Are you OK?"

"I'm fine," she gushed, chest still heaving, "I don't know what happened. I was sitting on the ladder, tied to the line, washing up just like you showed me; at least I think I was tied, but then—WOOSH! I was carried away! I'm so glad you were here!" She gave him an exuberant kiss on the lips and another wet embrace. He pushed her away, holding her at arm's length.

"Did the ocean take your swimsuit?"

"It did!" She laughed. "Can you believe it?"

She laughed. We had just rescued her from drowning in the high seas, miles from any coast or island. Saved from the awful, terrifying death that marks the punishment of an angry, cruel Neptune. It was something every man of the sea had considered at some time, and these thoughts and fears permeated his dreams. How long could he struggle to stay afloat, relying on his own energy to keep him above water? How long would he hold out hope for another vessel to come by that very fetch of water and find him? When would his body assume the chill of the water he was in? Until first his feet became numb and still, then his fingers, then legs. How long could he stave off the thoughts of hungry sharks finding him alone, defenseless? And how would it feel when, finally, weak in body and spirit, he let go of all hope and soundlessly slipped into the sea, allowing the cold, briny water to lap into his mouth and his throat, suppressing the urge to spit it out, to fight its quick progress, and instead, letting his lungs fill with water, pulling him down and swiftly carrying him off into the depths of the unknown? As sailors, we enjoy traveling the sea, but always remember our nature; man is not designed to live in the ocean. This is a truth made clear by a harsh and completely natural death.

Patty was oblivious to how close she had come to this miserable end. Was she that naïve?

I watched them standing together and a slow tightening began in my chest. What was going on with the two of them?

"Mate, take the helm," I commanded, making Leahy come away from Patty's ridiculous act.

"Yes, Captain." He moved over to me in a quick skip.

His brown arms dripped with water and the front of his white T-shirt and trousers were soaked through like he'd just come out of the sea himself. "Keep her steady now," I ordered.

Leahy took my place at the helm and looked at me with a question. With all hands securely on board, I took the rescue line he had used and made it fast to a rear stanchion. Hooking the loop in my hand, I climbed through the rails and dove into the surging sea. Hand over hand, I stroked up the nearest wave to retrieve the life preserver from where it still bobbed haplessly atop the next crest, watching over the sorry lot of us.

CHAPTER TWO

December, 1945
Leicester, Massachusetts

The world was only made of gray and white as a fast, early winter had shut out all other colors. It was quiet in the woods. A bird call was hardly heard; the wind was still. Our boots made the only regular sound as they crunched forward on hard, icy snow. Like our cheeks, the world seemed numb with cold. The first week in December and already we'd had two big snowstorms. The second piled snow upon the first and a good freeze hardened them together. It was the most snow Leicester had seen before Christmas in recorded history. The New England winter had begun, quick and harsh.

As boys, we didn't follow the almanac or worry about what this early storm might predicate for the coming months. School had been closed for three days. My father sat deep in his favorite chair, listening to the radio, the knees of his long legs pitched up before him like two tent poles, grouchy because he couldn't go to work. My mother was busy keeping up with my little brother, Jimmy. The house was feeling small and stuffy, and smelled like cooked cabbage. I was tired of making trips across the ice-crusted snow to the shed for more firewood. When I heard Ernie's boots on our front porch, I jumped up and ran to put on my warm clothes.

My mother met me at the door, smelling of baby powder and holding something behind her back. I knew what she was going to do. She looked at me with her sea-blue eyes and a smile on her face and presented the cumbersome long blue scarf.

"Don't run out without your scarf, Kenny." She wrapped it around my neck as I squirmed to look behind me through the window. Ernie was waiting on the porch, jumping up and down to stay warm. The scarf tucked in neatly, and having covered my ears and half my face, she was satisfied with the shield she had created. "Be home in time for supper. We're having corned beef, and I'm making a pie, too." She gave me a quick kiss on the cheek. "Stay warm!"

Within steps from the house the cold worked through my warm clothes. "Dang, it's cold out here!" I muttered. Even the mild wind we made as we moved seemed bitterly cold on my cheeks.

"Tell me about it!" Ernie said.

His wide brown eyes, framed in fair skin, pink in the cold, were all that showed. The rest of his head was wrapped up and covered like mine. Ernie was one year my senior and his family lived half a mile up the road. He had an adventurous spirit that matched my own. We both enjoyed exploring the woods and fields in the neighborhood, and as he was the only boy who lived nearby, we were best friends.

The forest had a thick canopy in summer, lending to little shrubbery on the ground. In winter we had a clear path among the tall trunks, standing like pillars in crooked rows. I stepped onto a log we often walked along the top of, a thick maple tree that had fallen years ago. The bark was slick with ice, and my feet slipped to and fro.

"Whoa!"

Ernie got up behind me, making the log bounce. "I'll bet you I can make it to the end without falling!"

"Big deal, me too!" We haphazardly made our way along the log and other snow-covered obstacles, finding our way through the forest bit by bit like regular National Geographic explorers. The world was white and quiet. It was unfamiliar to the eyes, but our ingrained sense of direction, honed from years of playing in this place, gave us the sense of knowing where we were. Instinctively, I knew my house was a distance behind us, and the main road into Leicester ran behind bushes and trees somewhere to the right. In the space between was a world of wonder. On warm summer days we unearthed bugs and worms beneath the leaf-strewn ground. Trees above cast their protective spells of shade and shadow, effortlessly protecting us from the heat, the noise, the world outside. We loved climbing onto fallen trees; their corpses made our own sort of jungle gyms. When a tree's bark became dry and flaky we pulled it off to discover ants busy at work. Sometimes they carried objects—a bit of leaf, or one time a group of them carried a dead spider, passing it hand over hand along the chain of ants. As soon as we thought we'd found their destination— There! Under the upturned root!—we would discover another trail of them headed off somewhere else. Following the ants, walking along fallen trees, and making up games as we went along, Ernie and I explored every corner of this stand of forest.

Now, a large field, smooth with snow, lay before us. It was free of trees or bushes. It looked completely strange to me. Had we wandered so aimlessly as to end up on unfamiliar ground?

"It's the pond!"

Indeed, he was right. The early winter had brought the pond to freezing; it was a slate covered in snow. In summer, it was a fine swimming hole, about twenty yards across and five feet deep. We could touch the bottom and wave our fingertips above the surface.

"It must be frozen solid under there."

"Has to be."

"Let's try it." A heavy stick in hand, Ernie tentatively pushed some snow away with his boot. White ice lay beneath. He gave the ice a tap. We heard a thick "thunk" sound. "Feels solid."

He scooted more snow away, and slid a foot forward. He did it again. In this funny shuffle he continued a yard or so. "Look, Kenny, it's like a block of ice out here!" I gently shuffled up alongside him, a few feet away. The ice felt thick, like it was a solid mass between us and the earthy pond bottom.

"Think I can make it across?" I asked Ernie, with a challenge in my voice.

"Maybe." He looked at the center of the pond, calculated for a minute. "It might be solid here, but I'm not sure about the middle."

"It's not too far; heck, I can almost jump across it."

He laughed.

We considered the pond. It wasn't too deep. It could be frozen through. After all, it had been really cold lately. And if it wasn't, you really only needed a good ten inches of ice to be solid. I was ten years old, I only weighed ninety pounds.

"I'm going to try," I said.

Ernie kept his place on the ice, a yard from the shore, walking stick in hand. He raised his eyebrows in an aloof manner. "I'll watch."

I crept out slowly, pushing the snow away with my boot to clear the ice. I wanted to see the surface below me, lest there were a bump, a hole, something to hamper my progress. I slid one foot ahead of the other, afraid a proper step might make it crack. But it was solid. It held my weight. I continued to move forward, nearing the center of the pond. Here I was, walking on water. I took my eyes from my treacherous path and looked up. The forest circled around me. I saw a mix of maple and beech trees holding snow on their fair branches, delicate and white, like my mother's crocheting. They stood calm, quiet, watching me. They were a beautiful, gentle trim around the gray sky above. I looked back at Ernie.

"All's fine out here! Come on!" I raised a hand and rose up on my toes in a manner of cheer. Coming down, my heels hit the ice with a firm tap. Then I heard the loudest sound of my short life—a crack like lightning was on top of us. Time stood still as I fell straight through. I saw the snow-covered trees above almost lean in to watch; my chest scraped the edge of ice before me. I smelled the water, sour and musty and full of autumn leaves. I went under. Suddenly my boots were swamped in chunks of ice. A cold rush wrapped my legs. My feet touched the bottom and I did the only thing I knew, I pushed hard and straight for the hole in the surface. I bobbed there, gasping for breath. My wet face felt like it was on fire in the cold air. In desperation, I reached out to clasp the gray sheet of ice before me. As I pulled myself up, it crumbled under my weight. I kicked beneath the water and moved my arms wildly, trying to stay afloat without anything to hold on to. The chill was capturing me; my arms were getting numb.

I didn't know the full effects of hypothermia but I did know I was in a bad spot. And my father was going to be furious. I saw his angry face in my mind's eye. "Don't ever challenge nature, Kenny, she always wins." How many times had he told me this? I knew better than to walk out on a pond, especially it not even being January yet. Every Boy Scout knows that.

My body was weakening, I couldn't stay afloat. I felt myself begin to sink.

"Kenny! Over here!" Ernie had his thick walking stick in hand, and taking aim, pitched it toward me. As my head went under, I stretched my hand up above the surface, miraculously catching the stick midair. I touched the bottom of the pond again, and tried to push myself back up. But my scarf was soaked with water, a heavy, cold weight around my neck. I could hardly move. My feet numbly kicked about, trying to push me upward. Then I felt a pull on the stick. I grabbed it with both hands, and kicking hard, moved with the momentum of the pull. My body came up and my chest crashed into the edge of the ice. It split and fell into the water.

Ernie stood at the edge of the pond, gripping the other end of the stick in two hands. "Hang on, Kenny, I'm going to pull again!" The fear in my best friend's face scared me.

"OK." I don't know if I said the words or imagined them.

He bent at the knees and leaned back with a strong tug. I tried to pull myself onto the ice, toward him, but again it crumbled. The ice was weakened with the cracks I made across its surface and the water was warming it, wearing it away. It wouldn't hold. My legs moved in slow-motion. I felt like I couldn't breathe. My body felt limp, tired. I wanted to close my eyes and rest. It was all I could do to keep my hands wrapped around the stick.

Ernie crept out on the ice where it was thick along the edge, moving in a low squat. He slowly lay down across the pond, the stick still connecting us.

"Hold tight!"

With a great heave he pulled me up onto the ice again. It held. For good measure he pulled me toward him once more. I slid on my belly across the frozen pond. We paused for a moment, lying face to face on the ice, exhaling hard white puffs of air. I couldn't feel the cold of the ice beneath me. I was completely numb.

"Let's get off of here!" He pulled me to my feet, and we made the final steps off the pond, the terrifying sounds of cracking ice behind us.

We turned to look. The ice we had just come across was gone. The brown surface of the pond rippled, gray shards of ice bobbed and dipped beneath the water. Another second and we both would have gone under.

I was shaking uncontrollably. Ernie removed my soggy coat and scarf and put his jacket around me. He pulled me by the hand through the trees toward the road; there would be no wandering through the woods on our way back.

All was quiet about, the icy road still and serene. Lined with snow-heavy trees and snowdrifts on both sides, the road seemed to be a tunnel of white, leading to a distant, even whiter sky beyond. We started hustling for home.

Luck was with us as a battered red truck soon pulled alongside. The driver must have taken pity on us as a sorry lot, Ernie coatless, dragging me at a bare limp behind him. The passenger door creaked opened.

Ernie pulled it wide open and looked in.

"Could we bother you for a ride, sir? My friend fell in the pond!"

"Get in, get in!" the driver cried. An old farmer, I think I recognized him from Coopers' dairy up in Rochdale.

Maybe the original Mr. Cooper himself. He was bundled in a thick coat, with a red knit hat pulled low over his forehead, and a red plaid flannel scarf wrapped high around his neck, covering his chin and mouth. We could only see his hard black eyes and pointy nose.

My body trembled against the thick solid bench of the truck seat. I was shaking hard. My teeth clattered. My fingers felt like popsicles, and I couldn't feel my toes at all. Is this what dying felt like? All I knew of the dead was what I'd overheard my father say of an old crotchety neighbor of ours—now he was "nothing but a frozen stiff on a cold slab at the morgue." I too was frozen stiff; my fingers were rigid, my flesh was pink and raw and goose-bumped like the chickens my mother plucked bare. Cold and meaty and dead to the touch. Was I freezing to death? Would they put me in a deep, cold, stony grave? Fears bounced through my mind, knocked about by the chatter of my teeth.

The farmer put the truck in gear and we moved forward, slowly. The old truck had a big wide windshield that was almost completely covered with frost, making it impossible to see through. The defrosting system was long broken, and he had replaced it with a small candle. About three inches high, stuck to the dashboard in its own melted wax, the candle made a warm glow on the glass, melting a hole in the frost. It was through this small, dim space, maybe ten inches across, that he peered, hunched low over the steering wheel, carefully navigating the icy road. The scent of fire and melting wax filled the cab. Ernie put his arm around me, trying to dull my shivering. I stared at the orange flame, so warm yet so small and far away. We crept along in this cautious fashion in the farmer's battered red truck. For better or worse, we were in his hands.

I awoke to my father's voice as he shook me roughly, "Kenny! Wake up, Kenny!" He scooped me into his arms and carried me from the truck into the house. In the middle of the kitchen my mother pulled off my shoes and stripped off my wet clothes, leaving them in a soggy pile on the linoleum floor. She hauled me to the bathroom, where she put me in the tub, filling it with a thick stream of warm water.

My father came to stand in the doorway.

"Dr. Russel's on his way."

Dr. Russel was the vet. He lived up the road just beyond Fritz Anderson's farm. I sat in the tub shaking in my near-frozen body, my fingers and toes tingling in the warm water. I could still feel the rush of falling; I shivered remembering the moment I'd gone overboard, sinking helplessly into the cold depths of the pond. My best friend Ernie had saved me from a wet, miserable death.

CHAPTER THREE

March 28, 1962
Location: 9° 12' 15" S
                138° 11' 03" W

At 0600 I came on deck for my morning weather check.
The sky was brightening as the early light peeked over the
horizon. A peach-colored band started there and spread
upward, where it faded into a pale yellow and then into the
still-dark part of the sky overhead. Venus shone above,
ready to disappear into the day. To the north no clouds
lined the horizon. It would be another fair, still day.

    I hated to leave the Marquesas after only three nights.
There was much more to see and explore about this set of
small islands, harbored thousands of miles from anywhere
else. It was a shame to leave so soon. But I couldn't linger;
I had made my decision, it was time to move on.

Two nights before, I sat alone on deck, docked in the Bay
of Traitors, watching the waning half-moon creep up above
the low hills on shore and keeping an eye out for my crew's
return.

In my mind I went through each of the steps and tasks of sailing the *Gracias*. As a two-mast schooner, there was double the work and planning. I thought about preparing the rigging, raising and unfurling the sails, and putting in and turned out reefs as needed. I imagined holding, cranking, or moving each apparatus or length of rope on her, in order, and sometimes simultaneously, with just my two hands. Some things could be lashed with a line, creating another pair of hands. I also had to consider the size of the sail and the power of the wind. Was I strong enough to adjust the sails if we were running full and by? In fair weather it was possible, but a storm could mean disaster.

I knew the *Gracias* to be as eager and willing as any ship, but my sail plans had not accounted for this situation. They were designed for an able crew of three for an around-the-world voyage. I would have to alter my rigging. The free sail was an inexact way to travel, but for a crew of one it was useful to provide time to rest. I would have to balance this against the time and effort it might take to tack back into the proper course.

Of course, many solo journeys had been accomplished before. I needed to only look below within my own bookshelf to see Joshua Slocum's *Sailing Alone Around the World*.

Captain Slocum circumnavigated the world alone in his beloved schooner the *Spray*, which he built himself with that journey in mind. It was in 1895 no less, and he relied on dead reckoning and a fragile clock that expired mid-voyage. In his telling he never seemed to fret about manpower. He spent many a leisurely day reading volumes of poetry and great novels as the *Spray* took him across this very ocean. With her long keel and his wise rigging, Slocum simply lashed the helm and let her go under a good wind, easily taking him two hundred miles a day, as he wrote long letters home with his fountain pen and sipped a cup of tea.

Slocum's story inspired unknown numbers of solo sailors. In his notes in the appendix, he gives a further nudge with this simple advice to sailors contemplating such a journey: "go." If you know the sea, he says, know that you know it, and remember it was meant to be sailed.

While I understood the technical and mathematical aspects of such a voyage, I was no Slocum; our collegiate regattas around the Sound at Kings Point were silly games compared to crossing this great ocean. Traversing the Pacific alone on my little forty-foot schooner would be a brand-new endeavor.

I considered my crew. While Leahy had worked hard to do his job and cover Patty's duties as well, I knew he wouldn't be able to keep it up. And that stunt she pulled—falling overboard! She put all of our lives in jeopardy with that ridiculous situation. Leahy might have proven to be an asset to the voyage, but Patty was clearly a liability; in my figuring, her faults brought the balance of the two of them far below zero. She was young and foolish. Really, she was a safety risk. Besides, I was sick of seeing her silly face.

These were my thoughts that night at Hiva Oa. Late in the night, when Leahy and Patty stumbled back aboard, I came to my verdict. I was done with the two of them. I'd make it better on my own.

Now, looking aft I clearly saw the peak of Mount Temetiu on Hiva Oa. She loomed large and foreboding, laughing at me still there in her sights and taunting me to return. In prideful determination, I turned my back toward her. I would never see that troubled soil nor the aptly named Bay of Traitors again. How I longed to take the *Gracias* immediately away from port, to sail hard and fast out to sea in that elation of waves crashing on the bow and salt filling the air, with victorious surges of wash left behind. To catch a good wind that carried me away from my troubles, and with distance, made my decision fast. Instead, we were becalmed.

I let out a sigh and resigned myself to the fate of my day and my choice; a slow drift north-by-northwest. Perhaps I would start working on the hammock I had in mind.

I solemnly adjusted my sails as I shaped my course now for Hawaii, rather than make the long Pacific crossing to the Society Islands, as I had once planned. By my estimates, the Marquesas to Hawaii crossing should take fifteen to eighteen days, twenty on the outside. It was a shorter, safer passage for a single-handed sailor.

And so it was that at Hiva Oa I left behind my crew, and with them my long-held dreams of the around-the-world voyage.

CHAPTER FOUR

August, 1954
US Merchant Marine Academy, Kings Point, NY

Set at the end of Long Island Sound, the US Merchant Marine Academy at Kings Point is a pretty place. You could easily forget you were only a few miles from the crowded, dirty city streets of New York. Kelly-green lawns stretched across wide expanses between brick buildings. The pathways were lined with elm trees, sharing the summer cheer of their bright green leaves as you passed under them. Evergreen shrubs were trimmed to dark green orbs along walls and steps. Little gardens of flowers decorated the corners of buildings and small courtyards. Beyond the grounds of this fancy estate was the marina. Boats bobbed there softly, one alongside the other, impossible to tell which mast belonged to which, their reflections mingling in the water. They seemed confident and pleased with their sharp bows and shiny rails, ready and waiting for whatever they were called to do next.

I was proud to be here, and I knew I was in good company. All around me I sensed the self-satisfaction of my fellow former class presidents and football team captains. It was no easy task to get into the US Merchant Marine Academy at Kings Point. The requirements included good grades, leadership abilities, a strong moral character, and the congressional nomination from your home state. My grades just made the minimum requirement, but I had been active in high school. Our principal, Mr. Jackson, was also my football coach, and it was because of him that I was here. Kings Point was his idea; he had a nephew who graduated recently and he thought it would be a good fit for me too. After talking with my father, he sent a request on my behalf to the offices of all fourteen of Massachusetts' representatives and both senators. One of them made the nomination and I submitted my application.

With our chests full and proud we lined up in the courtyard on our first day for our inaugural "muster." We had been issued our first uniforms; all wore the summer dress of denim trousers and blue chambray shirts. The day started with a tour of campus. A beefy third classman recited the history of the school and campus for us to memorize. Many years ago, this property was owned by Walter P. Chrysler, of car-manufacturing fame. A philanthropist and supporter of the maritime industry, he donated his estate to the government to found the Academy. His former home was now our administrative building, Wiley Hall. His front yard served as our fanciful quad, still beautifully manicured and bordered on one end with a reflecting pond overlooking the Sound.

Our guide also demonstrated how to walk "on the square," that is, in straight lines, turning only at exact right angles. Silly at first, like mechanical puppets, we gave each other covert winks as we turned sharp corners and pretended to walk on balance beams. This lost its charm as the day wore on, but this day was just the first. We were required to "walk on the square" as long as we were "plebes," foreseeably for the next ten months of our lives. Across campus, through buildings and in our classrooms, even in the locker room in the gym! It seemed like a silly and inefficient tradition for a military academy. But it was clearly something they took seriously.

The 0530 reveille came too soon. It seemed like I'd only been asleep for a few minutes.

I knew hard work from long summer days baling hay on Fritz Anderson's farm, when my body never stopped dripping with sweat and the back of my neck became scorched and peeling with sunburn. But this, this was something different. As first-year plebes, every moment of every day, and every aspect of our minds, bodies, and souls was to be consumed by this Academy. Day two was just beginning.

I pulled myself up out of bed and planted my feet firmly on the ground. Today we would begin classes. First, we had to get over to Delany Hall for our mess duties.

I heard the squeaky springs in the top bunk as my roommate rolled over.

"Already?" he complained.

"Yes, already."

I waited for him to come down the metal rungs at the foot of the bed before I got up. He stood and stretched, long arms almost hitting the walls on either side of our small dorm room.

Max was a tall, slim Italian from Chicago. He reminded me of a Great Dane puppy—he was excitable and all knees and elbows that bumped into the walls, the bed, and tipped over the desk lamp the first time he came in our room. I almost expected to see a tail, the way he could knock something over just by turning around. He called the top bunk right off, giving his long legs ample room to hang over the end.

We had only known each other for a day and I was slowly learning his language. He called girls "chicks," his suitcase was a "keister," a five-dollar bill was a "fin," and more than once he had already said, "Don't be a bunny, Bohlin"—his way of telling me not to be a fool.

He had dark hair and a quick smile and big nose. He told vivid, crazy stories about the gangsters and con men back in his neighborhood, pitching both eyebrows up into perfect right angles, with a "can you believe it?" look on his face. As he told a story, first the left eyebrow would fall back to a straight line, then the right, until he came to another exciting point, when they would both fly up once again. Far beyond me in his worldliness and mature demeanor, my hometown of Leicester, Massachusetts, was a place he could barely imagine. Max had a vision for his future bigger than any small town or grungy block of a big city. Disappointment crossed his face as he told me about his older brother Marcello, who began work in a television parts factory the Monday after his high school graduation. He and their father sat together in the lunchroom every noontime.

"No way, *Jose*! That's not for me. I know it's a long grind, and we're going to be lousy with work for the next four years. But I just can't see that kind of life. If I'm going to be working in a factory, I'm going to be upstairs!" Max took an interest in buildings and mechanics, and like me, had applied to Kings Point with plans to become an engineer. We were also alike in one of the quieter qualities of many Kings Point men; our parents didn't have the money to send us to college. For us, the seamanship part was secondary to our educations. Learning about boats was just part of the requirements to get a degree. At least that's one place I had a leg up on Max; I'd been in a few rowboats during camping trips at the lake. He'd never been on water in his life.

I didn't think it possible, but the "walking on the square" requirement endured while doing even the most agonizing plebe duty—serving mess to the midshipmen of the upper classes. Delany Hall was a long, rectangular, concrete block brick building. Rows of tall windows reached for the high ceiling along each wall. It felt as big as a football field. Dozens of tables stretched across the vast room, filled with hungry upperclassmen, all sitting with their companies. Their voices bounced off the walls, filling the hollowed space. We learned how to set up the trays and take them out to the mess hall, serving the first classmen first, and working our way down to the third classmen. They were a bunch of ingrates, every one of them.

"This is cold! Take it back!"

"It's about time. Can't you see we're all starved here?!?"

"What happened? This was a bacon and eggs in the kitchen—it turned to slop by the time you brought it out here! Speed it up, boy!"

The food looked OK to me. I didn't understand why the upperclassmen were so harsh. Eyes down, I hustled along quickly, rushing past their rough words, long white apron flapping against my shins and my black hard-bottomed shoes slapping the red brick floors.

When everyone was done we cleared away the dishes and were allowed to go back into the mess hall, tenderly walking "on the square" all along, and seat ourselves at those same tables and have our breakfast. After that, it was cleaning, instructions for when we were to return in the evening, and finally we were dismissed.

We hurried back to the dorm to dress in our formal "Summer White" uniforms and prepare for daily inspection. Having spent less than two days in a space half as big as my father's woodshed how could there be any mess? Yet this was a nerve-wracking task. During the training exercise the day before the stiff first classman in charge found six things wrong and we were each docked with three demerits. And that was during a practice run! I paid special attention to every detail this time. Our bunks were wrapped tightly with their blue wool blankets. The pillows lay neatly at the head, squared off and directly in the center. I used the length of my forearm as a ruler to be sure. Max worked on the dresser. He pulled out all of our clothes and folded them neatly. We had hastily unpacked when we arrived, shoving things into the drawers. This was the cause of many dings against our score. Who knew they would open the dresser to inspect the conditions inside? They were a picky bunch, for sure. We stood at attention in the hall outside our room while the first classman made his inspection. I was hot under my uniform. I began to sweat around my collar and armpits. He seemed to be taking forever. Was something wrong? Finally, he came out and gave us a curt nod; we had passed. I exhaled. We headed outside to the daily Presentation of Colors.

All midshipmen were present on the great lawn of Wiley Hall. Lined up in even rows in our stiff white uniforms, we stood holding our hats over our hearts. At the front of the formation a snare drum ratted out a quick beat and the rest of the band joined in. Heavy on brass and grounded with the deep boom from the bass drum, they launched into a lively version of *Stars and Stripes Forever*. The flag bearers marched forward carrying the flags of our country, the state of New York, and the Academy. In pairs, they unfolded each triangular bundle and raised it up its respective pole.

The flags picked up the early-morning breeze, and the band began *The Star-Spangled Banner*. All joined in to sing. The voices of the first classmen in the front rows carried across the lawn to us in the back. They sang loudly; these words were a pledge, a mantra, and a promise. The formality of the presentation was a frank reminder that we were at an Academy of the US Merchant Marines.

Back in our room I glanced at the clock. It was 7:15. I sat on the edge of my bunk, rested my elbows on my knees, and hung my head in my hands. It was overwhelming. Our schedules were filled to the brim; there was no time for blunders. There were dozens of things to do, every day. The list was endless. Besides learning our plebe duties, we had new terms to memorize, an impeccable level of cleanliness to achieve, fitness tests to pass, and new habits to master. Walking "on the square" alone was taking all of my focus. On top of that was our schoolwork. I was surrounded by valedictorians. Our instructors were naval officers. I was from a landlocked farm town where graduating from high school was considered an achievement, and I had never swum in the sea, much less sailed a boat upon it. What did I know about the Merchant Marines? I wasn't even the military type. My father never enlisted. We knew nothing of uniforms, commanding officers, or strict decorum.

I looked up as Max's long legs whisked by me. He went to the desk drawer and pulled out a notebook.

"Come on, Bohlin, the train is rollin'. Next stop"—he consulted the piece of paper in his hand—"Ocean Sciences!" He caught the look on my face. "Don't worry, man, our chores and the flags and all that stuff is done; this is the good part." He picked up my book bag from the foot of the bed and tossed it to me. "We gotta hustle, class starts in five minutes!"

My worries fell away during my first hour in Ocean Sciences.

The room was old and warm. Great molded pillars held up the ceiling and the early sun came through tall windows. We sat in wooden chairs with small desks attached, chatting with our neighbors.

I had just met BJ, the plebe sitting on my right, when a collection of emphatic "Shhh!" sounds moved through the room. Unbeknownst to many of us, the professor had begun class. Lt. Carney was a stout, serious man. He wore glasses, and had thick, arching eyebrows over bulging eyes. As time went on, I learned they created a dramatic effect whether he was explaining tragedies at sea or his grading policy. But today, they drew us all in to his story.

"That's right, men," he continued in a soft voice that made us lean in, "your ship is like a terrarium."

A terrarium? The thing Cousin Ginger had on her bedroom windowsill? I looked around. The young class was rapt by this concept, each man sitting forward in his seat, not wanting to miss a word. He went on to explain.

"It contains your entire world. You have your varieties of fuel on board, each used for different purposes. Like the sun and the soil, which feed your plants in their own, appropriate ways. Your fresh water supply is held on board; it is limited and used with the utmost prudence. Not unlike the water that accumulates on the glass to carefully irrigate the plants in your terrarium. And you, gentlemen, you are the bugs, the worms, the frogs you chose to populate this world. On board you are a collective, captive entity. You have your own society, so to speak. Someone will be in charge. Others will follow their orders. With this, you have all the tools you need to complete your voyage, much as the frogs succeed at living in their world, encapsulated in the terrarium. You have the means to keep your vessel safe, to stay healthy and whole, and make your way as you desire. With the proper planning, training, and attitude, you can take your boat, indeed, your world, around the planet and visit the many different countries, cultures, and people on this great sphere we live on, Planet Earth."

Not a plebe moved; we all sat silent, amazed at his words. BJ caught my eye, a huge grin on his face. Was this what we had in store? A journey around the world?

"Now, having said that, it will take a great deal of effort and dedication on your part to be ready for such a journey, to prepare your terrarium, if you will. I will assume I have your utmost commitment, until you show me otherwise. Let's get to work." He turned to the blackboard and began writing.

Until this moment, I never thought of my education at Kings Point in those terms. It was a means to get out of Leicester, a way to have a better life than my father's before me. But to learn the skills to sail the world? To possibly have my own boat? My own world, for traveling about on this one? It sounded pretty keen to me, a boy who never had his own room to sleep in, much less his own world to travel the planet. I'd better figure out this Academy thing pretty quick.

CHAPTER FIVE

March 29, 1962
Location: 9° 55' 03" S
             139° 05' 26" W

We finally moved past the tiny islands spewed around the Marquesas to the open sea. Nothing lay between the *Gracias* and the horizon, not a reef nor spit of rocks in any direction. I enjoyed the freedom here, alone. At sea level on deck, my view was limited to about four miles, but it felt like a hundred. The ocean seemed to stretch to infinity in all directions. Nothing stood in our way, the world was mine as far as I could see. It was all there for the *Gracias* and I, in every direction.

The morning sun was a relief. I'd had a fitful night's sleep. Just as I was nodding off I'd jolt awake—had I heard voices? Waves crashing on a nearby shore? Was the *Gracias* in harm's way? I would jump up and head on deck, my eyes quickly scanning the sea before I'd even cleared the companionway. After going through that exercise a few times, I brought a pair of cushions up from a salon bench and camped on deck the rest of the night. From there I could easily sit up, assure myself that we were still miles from any shore or ship, and sink back into sleep.

During the day I was getting along just fine. I was managing the lines and the sails, sometimes tying something down with another length of line to hold it in place while I reached for something else. I found that the twine lashings I'd made to mark my lines were accurate sometimes, but during the first few days of slow going I made many adjustments. Along with my daily coordinates, I kept records in the log about the weather, wind direction, sail position and trim. I decided it prudent to take detailed notes on what I had done or not done. I was completely reliant on myself to make this journey. There was no one to help me remember what happened the day before. I found it fun to improvise, and create techniques to do it all on my own. Necessity, as they say, is the mother of invention.

The wind picked up, and with it, so did my mood. I began to feel excited about this journey again. My original plans had gone awry; and my second effort, with Leahy and Patty, had been a failure. But I was continuing on anyway. I felt inspired by a new challenge: to travel the Pacific single-handed.

Past experience taught me that in the serendipity of sea travel, amazing things happen. You will visit places you have only imagined in your mind, where you will meet and befriend people you never knew existed. Somehow, it is always a surprise to find that, like you, they have been going about their lives half a world away, in the unique and varied ways of their own culture, trade, and customs. Yet in the moments of a brief conversation you will find their hopes and aspirations are no different than yours. On the waterfront especially, which is generally made up of tolerant and cosmopolitan men, you will become an immediate, dear, and lifelong friend of a man of another language and religion. You will be such kindred comrades that you cannot imagine never having known him, even if, for your entire life up until then, you could hardly have imagined his existence. This is the life of following the stars and currents of these great seas. I looked forward to the adventures ahead.

Sailing alone wasn't my first choice, but I was determined to make the best of the decision I'd made. It would be a quick run, a couple of weeks; I could manage it just fine.

CHAPTER SIX

December, 1955
New York

I pulled the collar of my coat up around my ears. My knit
cap was pulled down as far as it could go and still allow me
to see. I smelled the cold. Water turned to ice without a
hint of earth. Spits of snow drifted around me, the ground
was frozen solid, and it was pitch dark. I was going to need
a bit of luck to be seen standing here in this deep-navy
Academy-issued coat. It was warm as a barn but not too
helpful for nighttime hitchhiking. The dress shoes were
useless for the task as well. Hard black leather with the
thinnest of soles that slipped on any bit of ice. The Winter
Blues, they called this uniform. You can imagine the jokes
we made with that.

Just another hundred and fifty miles. Cy had dropped
me here before heading to his folks in Upper Nyack. We'd
finished our fall semester finals earlier that afternoon, tidied
our rooms until they were near sterile, jumped in his car,
and got the heck out of the city. I was hoping to pick up a
ride on the Thruway. Truckers were the best guys to catch

rides with. They were all business and didn't lollygag with stops and socializing. They wanted to get where they were going so they could start from there and get to where they were going all over again. If I caught a ride with the right driver I could be home by midnight.

My toes were nearly cubes of ice when I saw the headlights of a big rig easing onto the shoulder. I tossed my duffel across my back and ran up to his cabin door. The window was a black impenetrable sheet. The driver lowered it, one crank at a time. Ice frozen along the frame hampered his progress. Eventually I saw a scraggly beard and the rim of the trucker's cap. His eyes were hidden in the shadows. His voice carried down to me.

"Mighty cold night for a stroll. Where ya headed?"

"North, sir. Leicester, Mass, to be exact. Or anywhere nearby would be fine."

"You in the service?"

"At the Merchant Marine Academy, sir. Kings Point. Second year."

"Very well, come aboard, sailor."

I got lucky that night. He was headed to Quebec, with no stops planned along the way. The driver was happy to give me a ride and I was happy to keep him company. The cab was warm and I relaxed back into the soft seat.

"Been anywhere exciting?"

"Not yet. Just around the Sound, up the coast. Haven't seen much besides my books and my bunk. Next semester we go to sea. How about you?"

"Well, I can say I've seen almost all of these lower forty-eight, and much of Canada. What do you study down there, besides sailing?"

"We're training to be officers in the Merchant Marines."

"What's that do?"

"Well, for one, I'll be able to command ships that take cargo all over the world."

"We kinda have the same job then."

"Yes, sir, I suppose so."

He gave a nod and continued to stare out at the road ahead, silent for the next ninety miles. I left him to his solitude and watched out the window, wishing it were daylight so I could measure my return to New England. I knew in the pitch darkness miles of forests ran in every direction. The land softened as we moved away from the coast, into rolling hills and farmland.

Maybe it was out of pity on this cold dark night, or perhaps it was the first act of kinship I received from a fellow international transporter, but the truck driver silently took me almost ten miles out of his way to the heart of Leicester. At the junction of Main and Paxton he brought the truck to a rest. His headlights lit up the gas station ahead of us, the only building in sight.

"Thank you for the ride, sir, you sure helped me out."

"Yep," he said. "You'll be OK here?" he added, surveying the dark empty street. We were at a rural crossroads in the middle of farming country. There were no other cars; no lights twinkled in any direction.

"Yes, sir, my father will fetch me."

"Alright then. Safe travels, my boy."

I turned to look over my shoulder before hopping out of the cab. "Same to you, sir. And many thanks for the ride."

He shut the door behind me before my feet hit the ground, already ready to be on his way.

Gimondi's Gas Co. was long closed. I looked at my watch—a quarter past midnight. Sorry, Mr. Gimondi. I went around the garage to the house and knocked on the door of the screened-in porch. There was a rustle inside, a bang, and suddenly I was aglow in the porch light. The door to the house opened, and Mr. Gimondi stepped forward and peered at me through the glass door of the porch.

"Yo, Kenny? That you?"

"Yes, sir."

"Come in, come in." He went to unlatch the door and let me onto the porch. It was about half a degree warmer there.

"Well, I'll be. Look what the wind blew in. Marty said you'd be coming home soon."

"Yes, sir."

"Mondi?! Who's there?" a woman's voice called from inside the house.

"Alice, it's Kenny, Marty's boy. He's had a long night, by the looks of him."

I could only look down to hide my smile. Mr. Gimondi was known for his slick black hair and wearing smart Italian suits behind the register and even as he pumped gas. Tonight his hair was a mess of sticks from resting on his pillow, and an old robe was thrown around his shoulders, exposing faded flannel pajamas beneath.

"Well, I'm sure he wants to get home to his folks, don't keep him waiting out there."

"Oh, yeah, that's right. Want me to give your dad a ring, Kenny?"

"Yes, please. That would be great."

"Will do, right-o." He disappeared back into the house.

I waited on the porch, trying to stay still and not disturb the Gimondis any further by stamping my feet. Finally, the headlights of my dad's 1946 Crown Imperial turned into the gas station.

He stepped out of the car and in two long strides met me in the middle of the deserted station. He put his arms around me, slapped his hands against my back.

"Picked a cold night to come, didn't you?" He stood back, arms on my shoulders, assessing my face.

"Sure did, Dad, let's get outta here."

After a busy week of challenging final exams and a cold, long journey mostly reliant on the kindness of strangers, at that late hour you would think I would have enjoyed a hot shower and collapsed into bed. But it wasn't that way. As was my habit, regardless of the hour, after bathing I sat at the kitchen table and ate the meal my mother prepared me. Tonight it was my favorite homemade chicken soup, leftover mashed potatoes, canned green beans from the summer garden, and her blackberry pie. As I ate I regaled my folks with stories from school, with all the enthusiasm and charm that comes naturally to a young country boy fresh from the city. At that warm hearth I told funny and damning stories of my professors and my classmates. I told them about BJ's latest antics and Max's engineering project. I shared the fascinating theories and practical applications of math and science I had learned. I told tales of Neptune and his unconditional authority over the great sea. As my little brother and sister lay fast in their bunks, I enjoyed my home-cooked meal and we shared many hearty laughs until long after the first rooster crowed. From time to time my father stifled a yawn and refilled his coffee cup. My kind mother's bright sea-blue eyes never dimmed, but stayed on me, as she absorbed my every word.

CHAPTER SEVEN

April 1, 1962
Location: 1° 01' 28" N
            138° 09' 13" W

The *Gracias* and I were having a fine day. Sometime in the night we had crossed the equator again, and now southerly winds were pushing us along at a good clip, at least eight knots. Feeling the wind in my hair and the sun on my bare chest I stood at the helm with a smile on my face. Now this was sailing! The *Gracias* moved out smoothly, sails bellied, enjoying a full wind. I swore she was smiling too. All around us was deep, dark blue ocean. Despite the wind, the seas were calm, and we easily slipped over each small crest as the current pulsed below us. There was not a cloud in the sky above. Yes, this sea was meant to be sailed.

The sun was now almost directly overhead and there was a rumble in my stomach. Had so many hours passed as I stood here, holding her steady? We had been cruising smoothly for so long the small splash from the starboard rail surprised me. Maybe a rogue bit of wave. Moments later a spray of saltwater splashed my face. In the water there I saw a dark gray shadow. A fish of some kind, moving with us, keeping pace with the boat. Another spray came across the deck and this time I looked quickly enough to catch a glimpse of gray shiny skin and a sliver of dorsal fin. It sank back into the water and I saw a second shadow beside it. The shadow moved to come up out of the water, taking a smooth leap over the surface and then back down with a squeak of its beak. Porpoises!

They were matching the *Gracias'* pace, swimming on her starboard side. At least a dozen of these marvelous creatures came alongside, alternating turns at jumping up out of the water. Long and lean and all forward motion, one hopped up, easy as a deer springing over a fence, and slipped back into the sea. As soon as its nose touched the water another flew forward, taking its turn at a jump. In this way they progressed among the set of them, up and down and back and forth like a piano player hitting the keys in perfect succession.

The wind was holding steady, but as a precaution I reefed the sails. These were the first friends I had seen in days. I didn't want to miss a thing. Lunch could wait. I locked the tiller at the helm and went to the forward storage compartment where I dug through my diving gear and pulled out my mask and snorkel.

My little pod of friends had doubled. There were at least two, maybe three dozen sleek gray forms rising and falling through the air all around the *Gracias* at varying intervals like the horses on a merry-go-round. Several moved forward and, keeping pace with the *Gracias*, made a weaving pattern across her bow and back again in an intricate dance with her and each other. It was a wonder to watch.

I secured a line around my waist and wrapped the end around a cleat. I wanted to see more of this. With the

Gracias heeling slightly port, I lay down on my stomach on the forward port deck and shimmied over the edge until my torso stuck out above the water. I pulled down my face mask and fell forward, folded at the waist. My ankles were wrapped around the upright stanchions, holding me half onboard. My face and shoulders in the rushing water, I twisted my body to face aft. My snorkel just cleared the surface. At first I only saw a stream of bubbles from the boat's wake. I put out my hand to block the water trailing off the *Gracias* and my view cleared. Now I could get a closer look.

They were even more elegant under water. In a rich blue background lit by the direct noon sun, the whole school of them were swimming toward me, dark gray forms spotted with sunlight, dipping and diving with the flows. Their powerful tails propelled them smoothly in any direction they chose. They shot up toward the surface, and on re-entry spun their entire bodies around, somersaulting in a complete circle, maybe even two, just for the fun of it. A pair broke off, rolling around each other, then blending back into the group. I tried to keep my eye on each of them, to follow their actions and discern one from another. But they were as sly as a pack of magicians, distracting me with their charming moves as they swam about, craftily maintaining their anonymity. Like children at play, they seemed to completely enjoy themselves and each other.

One took a sudden turn to swim out of the pack and toward me, wondering at my dangling presence. It came up to me directly, not twelve inches from my mask, and took me in with its strange, monocular eye. It seemed to have a slight smile the way the line of its mouth curled upward; it looked like a friend, not foe. The length of a human, it had a dark gray upper body and a lighter, almost white belly. I must have been a wonder to it, half a human form submerged in its universe, traveling along at a brisk eight knots, with no effort at all on my part. After a moment of swimming alongside, studying me, it seemed to give a nod of acknowledgment, then zipped ahead. I twisted forward in time to see it do a complete somersault, allowing perfect timing for the pod to catch up, whereby it was scooped back into our moving party under the sea.

Shortly, another friend swam up to visit. When it was done looking me over, it spurted forward, took a quick jump out of the water, and fell back into the pod as we moved through. Another came to look me over, then another. This went on for the next several minutes, each of them taking a turn at inspecting me. I couldn't tell if they were each different creatures, or if one or two had snuck back into the rotation for a second or third look. They were quick, and nearly identical in color and form. Visiting me this way seemed to be a fun game to them, and I wished I could participate with more than a smile and a small wave. It was tempting to reach out to touch them, their smooth skin just an arm's length away. But they kept a fair distance between us and I respected their boundary. Who knew how sharp the teeth of these little mammals could be? I certainly didn't want to leave a stream of bloody water behind.

They continued on with the *Gracias*, full of vim and vigor, mindless of the hour or the distance they traveled. It felt like no time had passed at all, but my knees and ankles began to ache, and my hunger had returned; it was long past lunchtime. I waved what felt like a lackluster good-bye in the midst of their natural grace, and hauled myself up.

It has been said that a porpoise is akin to man in his intellect. After witnessing this I would agree. They moved with the precision of any military corps, and had impeccable timing. It may have been innate, but who's to say they didn't plan it on the fly? Many a Kings Point cadet could learn a thing or two from them. They are joyful creatures too. Never before had I seen wild animals let loose like sailors on leave in a dance hall. They spun and jumped and danced among themselves for no reason but for the pure joy of it. Within the pod I also sensed a genuine affection. They didn't compete; I heard no arguing or grumbling among them either. They were happy with themselves and each other. Their warmth and companionship filled the water like the joy of a church congregation singing a happy hymn, hearts light and full of affection. What a state to live in.

As far as I could tell, the *Gracias* had held her course and we were still headed north-by-northwest. At sunset I brought out the sextant. My guess was right; we had traveled a direct path for eleven hours today. The *Gracias* flew perfectly straight, even as I hung my head in the sea. I knew she would be true, from the first moment I stood at her helm and held the thick wooden tiller in my hands. I was lucky to have her.

Pleased with the progress of the day and still feeling elated from the visit of my porpoise friends, it came to mind I was so busy reveling in the fun I forgot to set out my troll line. Just like lunch, it would be a dinner of canned chili, heated on my little stove, with a side of very ripe papaya. After eating I washed the dishes, stowed the pot and bowl in their respective homes, and tidied the galley. The boring meals didn't bother me. Today was as perfect a day as one could ask for. I was living a good life.

The quick twilight of the equator fell around me as I hastened to string up my new hammock between the main mast and rail at the bow. I climbed in with my flashlight and book. Wrapped in a blanket, I opened *Flash, the Lead Dog*, my childhood favorite. It never failed to entertain me with its tale of two young men and their adventures crossing the Canadian wilderness. Here their ambition led them to travel by dogsled and on foot through great valleys and across vast plains of snow and ice in search of game and valuable furs. They hunted moose and elk to feed them and their dogs, and all manner of furs, including fox, mink, and rabbit. In the blackest of deep winter nights, they relied only on the stars and themselves for survival. They slept in makeshift berths dug in deep pockets of snow, lined with pine boughs and layers of animal skins. Wrapped in an assortment of pelts, they tried to stay warm enough to sleep through the night. Their loyal pack dog, Flash, tucked himself cozily between them.

My bed at sea was quite fair by comparison. Here I lay, strung up in a hammock of my own making, swaying in the temperate breeze, out on the open water with a full view of the constellations above. The only thing lacking was the warm affection of a faithful dog to keep me company. Content with my day, and unconcerned about the future, I fell into a deep dreamless sleep beneath the stars.

CHAPTER EIGHT

April, 1957
Kings Point, New York

BJ eased the rudder slightly, and the little S-Boat came abreast of the dock. I hopped off with the bowline in my hand and wrapped it snuggly around the cleat on the pier. I moved aft.

"Think fast!" BJ tossed me the aft line; I reached out behind me and caught it blindly midair.

"You never miss, do you?"

"What's to miss? It was right there." I gave him a grin and made the line secure. "Let's get this hot rod put away before Delany closes," I said, and hopped back on board.

"Yeah, I've got to refuel."

"Me too."

The sail fell, and between the little boat's rigging and mast I saw the light puff of clouds and pink sky above the sound. Sailing here in the early evening I often forgot I was near one of the biggest cities in the world. Out on that expanse of water all was calm. Despite any wind or waves, it was quiet there, in a way the city never would be.

We were both on the Windjammer Racing team, and every spring, three days a week, we practiced after classes in preparation for our Saturday regattas. I liked sailing with BJ. We tried a variety of experiments with the rigging in an effort to maximize our speed. It could be a rough ride in an afternoon gale, but we weren't concerned with comfort. Just winning.

We set about neatly putting away the sail, he at one end of the boom, me at the other. BJ and I both subscribed to the Academy's rules that echoed those of my own father: a place for everything, and everything in its place. It was important to be tidy onboard. For safety's sake and for the fact that the little boat wasn't more than a skiff out on the water. Any clutter left on the small deck could trip you right over and spill you into the drink.

"I can't wait until we get our own boat, Ken. I want a teak interior, and the decks too. Durable, and they look handsome." BJ had sailed all his life, on a variety of boats, and of all the striking memories he had he always went back to having everything teak, inside and out.

I was a bit more practical. "Yeah, I know, the teak deck. I want something big, and fast." I saw myself at the helm, wind on my face, moving my boat with ease, by and full. "I know we want to take our time visiting places, but I sure hope we can beat some records too."

"We will! No need to take our time during the crossings!" He handed me the end of a line, I coiled it up in a tight loop, over shoulder and elbow, until it was a neat bundle. All ship-shape, we made our way out of the marina and straight for the mess hall. The darkening sky told me we had only a few minutes to make it through the door before they closed at seven.

Over supper we went on, listing all the fabulous places we would visit. The great dining hall was almost empty but for a few stragglers like us. BJ wanted to go back to Indonesia and Thailand, where he had sailed during our sea year. He spoke of the amazing green waterways and little specks of rocks that served as islands throughout. I wanted to see them as well. And the great cliffs of Tasmania. And Australia and New Zealand, of course. The list was endless. We had both read Captain Slocum's *Sailing Alone Around the World,* and it had tickled our imaginations. There was so much to see on this great earth, and what better way than on a sailboat with your best mate? If things went awry, as they ultimately did for Slocum, well, what was more romantic than that? To have "Lost at Sea" etched on our tombstones wouldn't be such a bad ending. We called our plan "The Worldwide Tour."

"What if it's not just the two of us?" BJ said, suddenly sounding serious. "What if we want to bring someone else along?"

"Like Kepler?" He was on the Windjammer team with us. "Or Scottie? He'd be a hoot."

"Sure. Maybe one of them. Or…" He finished chewing the big bite he'd stuffed in his mouth and looked at me. "You know after we graduate we have our active duty commitment."

"Sure."

"And after that we'll have to work a few years to save up some money. We'll be gone, working at sea, two, three years."

"Right."

"And with the route we're planning and the stops we want to make, we'll be away another three, four years, right?"

"Maybe longer!"

"Right." He took a deep breath. "It's just that it's a long time to ask a gal to wait."

"A gal? Which one?"

"You know, Jean. We've been going steady almost a year now."

"She's the one from Rhode Island?"

"Yeah."

"OK, Jean. You're really on the hook with her, aren't you?"

"I guess you could say that."

"Does she sail?"

"I've taken her out on the water a few times, she likes it. I told her all about our plans; I think she'd be game to join us. I could teach her some things. She'd make herself useful, I know she would. She's a great gal, Ken." His eyes locked on mine. "And if I go away for so long, I might lose her to someone else."

BJ was committed to our plan but I saw the conflict he was facing. "Are you going to propose?"

"I think I might have to." He smirked.

"Then you better teach her to sail."

"I think I need to buy a ring first."

I laughed. "Yeah, she's going to want one of those. You think she'll be able to endure The Tour? It's a long journey. Three of us on a boat. No hair salons or shopping with the girls. Just us guys."

"I think she'll love it. But I've got to ask her the other question first."

As we went on, we felt the eyes of the hungry plebes standing along the walls, waiting for us to finish so they could clear our plates and eat themselves. We shoveled in the rest of our meal as quickly as we could. After almost four years we had matured to see ourselves as benevolent first classmen, taking pity on the fourth class. We couldn't lollygag anyway, we had homework to do.

As I studied late nights, I often looked at a slip of paper I had taped on the wall above my desk. It was a quote from my favorite childhood author:

> *"Twenty years from now, you will be more disappointed by the things you didn't do than those you did. So throw off the bowlines. Sail away from safe harbor. Catch the wind in your sails. Explore. Dream. Discover."*—Mark Twain

It was exactly what I planned to do.

There is nothing more glorious than a full summer's day at Kings Point. Trees shimmer in boundless health and sunshine. Every walkway seems to lead you through a small forest designed to cast its cooling shade over you. A refreshing breeze comes off the Sound. Smooth and silvery, the water captures small shadows in the current, like the brief darkness inside a spoon. Summer days at Kings Point will put you in the mind of a leisurely visit to a fine estate. You might expect a neatly dressed butler to appear before you with a tray of sparkling drinks.

As first classmen, we left much of the hard work to the plebes, but we were responsible for the tedious inspections. They gave all the boats a good cleaning, inside and out. We made sure all was orderly on board and on shore. As we were reminded by every officer who walked by, the campus, and especially the marina, had to be flawless. "Spic-and-span, men, spic-and-span!" Not a flake of dirt or a streak of grease was to show anywhere. We would be having important visitors, and more than a few of them had an eye for such detail. At the end of the week we were proud of her; our campus shone like a new penny.

I was looking in the mirror, straightening my collar, ensuring I, too, was "spic-and-span" for today. There was a knock on my door.

"Yeah?" I called over my shoulder.

"Hey, Bohlin." BJ opened the door, hat in his hands, and stuck his head through the entry.

"Hey, BJ."

The smell of Old Spice followed him into the room. "You ready, buddy?"

"Almost. Just putting the final touches on here."

He laughed. "Looking sharp, sailor!"

I straightened my hat and he joined me before the mirror. We stood side by side, the same height, the same slim build. We were virtually twins in our dress whites. Under our hats our hair was tightly trimmed with fresh Navy-issued haircuts and you couldn't see the discrepancy between the colors. Only our eyes looked different. His were a deep, thoughtful brown; they seemed somber this morning. He looked at me in the mirror.

"Did you ever think we'd make it to today?"

"I knew I would, I wasn't so sure about you." I turned to face him and we both laughed. "I'm going to miss this place. It's been some good times, hasn't it?"

"Yes, it has. But our work here is done, it's time to start looking toward the future." His serious look returned. "You're still game for The Tour?"

"You know I am. Give us a couple of years, and then the world awaits!" I slapped a hand on his shoulder. "And right now, I know Jean and your folks are waiting for you. Let's go."

The graduation ceremony was held on the great lawn in front of Wiley Hall. Sitting under the sweltering August sun in my summer whites, I went back and forth between listening to the inspiring speakers and looking around me. I remembered the sense of pride I had my first day here. Now again I was in good company. These were good men who were smart, well trained, prepared, and above all else, honorable. I was glad to have come to know them over the years, and I'd be happy to be at sea with any one of them.

After the ceremony, I made my way through the crowd of graduates with their families. I saw a head above the crowd and headed in that direction. There was my father, mother, my brother Jimmy, and my little sister Kathy. With them were my uncle Austin, my grandmother, and our neighbors, the Andersons.

My father stepped forward from the group and put out his hand. His grin stretched wide. We shook hands and he pulled me in for a hug. "I'm proud of you, son!" He held me tight, and I knew he meant it.

"Thanks, Dad."

I turned to my mother beside him. I looked down into her happy, smiling face. Her hair was done in neat dark curls and she wore a new summer dress. She clutched the ceremony program in one hand and a tissue in the other. I reached down to give her a hug. Her small, round frame was warm through her dress and she smelled like roses at the end of summer. Her hands on my shoulders, she came up on her toes to whisper into my ear. "He's so proud of you Kenny. I am too." There was a tingle in the corners of my eyes and soon they were damp. I was glad to know I had made my parents proud.

I saw her slide a tissue under her glasses to wipe at the tears pooling under her eyes. I hugged her again. She patted my back.

"It's OK, Kenny, say hello to the Andersons."

I wiped my eyes with the back of my hand and turned to shake hands with Fritz Anderson. Mrs. Anderson gave me a hug. Their son, Eric, shook my hand.

"Good for you, Kenny. I can't believe we have a Kings Point graduate, from little Leicester, Mass. Nice job!"

My brother, Jimmy, shook my hand next, and I pulled him close for a hug too. Small arms wrapped around my waist from behind. Little Kathy. I picked her up and swung around in a circle. She screamed and laughed.

I was happy to have my family there, small as it may be, and honored that our longtime family friends had come all the way to see me too. Motioning us all together, Eric stepped back until he had us all in his sights and snapped a photo.

That night after supper my father came into the bedroom I would be sharing with Jimmy. I was unpacking my bag, filling a dresser drawer with my small assortment of clothing. I planned on staying in Leicester for a few weeks before I shipped out from Annapolis in September.

It surprised me when he shut the door behind him.

"This came for you yesterday."

"What is it?" I glanced over my shoulder.

He held out a plain white envelope with my name and home address printed in small, almost childlike handwriting.

"Who's it from?" I took it, glancing at the back for a return address. It was blank. I looked again at the front, the postmark on the American flag stamp said Tampa, Florida.

"If I had a guess I'd say it's from your mother."

We stood facing one another, looking into each other's eyes. While we had always shared the same round Swedish face and pairs of ears that stood out like flags in the wind, I was finally as tall as him too. I saw his eyes were a perfect reflection of mine, a calm and clear steel-gray blue. I looked down at the envelope. My mother. It felt like the pieces of a jigsaw puzzle had all spilled out onto the floor between us. Memories and blank spaces tumbled around in my mind.

"I know I haven't told you much about her, Kenny. I guess I wanted to spare you some of that unpleasantness. You've probably heard a thing or two. Leicester's a small town, and word travels from Worchester too. The kindest thing I can say about her is she was young and foolish." He shook his head. "Don't ever let a woman be your downfall, Kenny. You'll hate yourself if you do." He sighed. "But she gave me you. A son is the best thing to happen to a man. We may have had a rough start in the beginning, but your mother, Phyllis, that is, always loved you like her own. She's taken good care of us both. Whatever this letter says, don't forget that."

I nodded. We never talked about it, but I had known the woman with the bright sea-blue eyes I called my mother didn't give birth to me. I had memories of that winter when we lived with my dad's sister, Aunt Caroline, and her husband, Uncle Gino. I was excited to live with my cousins. Bobby was eleven, and I followed him around trying to do all the things big boys like him could do. Ginger was eight, and she gloried in the chance to be a doting older sister. She had a cat too, a pure white one they called Snowball. They lived in a great big two-story house with a staircase that overlooked the front room. It had a smooth, wide banister we slid down when the grown-ups weren't looking. But for all the fun we had, I knew my dad was sad over those cold, long months.

I myself felt a dooming sense of worry in that house. Could my mother find us living here? I hoped she remembered Aunt Caroline's address. She had already been gone longer than all the other times. But she said she'd come back; that's what she told me. I'd clung to that memory.

Now I was looking at the unfamiliar handwriting of this woman. I had just finished school and I had big plans for my future. I had made commitments, signed agreements, and made arrangements in a long line of events. I was at the starting gate and ready to shoot forward with the mere turn of the calendar. Would her words change my plans, my future, and my life?

I opened the letter. It was short, considering the years that had passed.

"Dear Kenny,

I hear from a friend in Worchester that you are set to graduate from a Marine Academy. She says it's a prestigious thing, so I guess congratulations are in order. I knew you were a smart boy, from the first time I held you. You must also have a bit of my Scottish pluck in you to make it through. I suppose your father wouldn't like to hear that. I'm proud a son of mine has accomplished so much.

I hear Phyllis keeps a good house and you have a brother and a sister now. I don't really have time for that. You see, life has taken me on a turn or two. There's so much fun to be had here. In Florida we enjoy warm weather year-round. I'm grateful not to suffer from those dreadful Massachusetts winters.

All my best,

Your mother (Helen)"

She was proud of me? Why? She hadn't done one thing to help me through school, or in any other part of my life. It was like she was taking credit for my accomplishments. And "Scottish pluck?" It made me think the rumors I had heard about her were true. "A wild dame," to use Max's lingo. She still sounded young and foolish. What a lovely life she must have, so busy in her heavenly Florida she couldn't be bothered with her son in Massachusetts. I handed the letter to my father to read and turned back to my unpacking.

Her words hadn't changed my plans after all, but made them resolute.

CHAPTER NINE

April 4, 1962
Location: 1° 01' 28" N
            138° 09' 13" W

I watched the red dash of the floater bobbing against the darkest blue ocean. Other than that speck of red, my world was a monochromatic field of blue, broken only by a faint line between the sea and sky. The water lay before me like a great drape of blue silk, a shimmer here, and a curl of deep color there. Low cumulus clouds spread in a neat row along the horizon, flat along their bottoms and topped with little puffs of white, the sky behind them an opaque, pale blue curtain. Everything was a shade of blue. And the bright red floater, softly balanced there.

I'd decided to throw out my line while the *Gracias* waited for wind. At dawn all was still, the sea calm. I suspected I had run into the ITCZ. Consulting my charts, it looked like indeed I had fallen into the heart of the Intertropical Convergence Zone, or in laymen's terms, the doldrums. The current that ran just north was what I wanted; it was a straight shot to Hawaii. But here I was stuck. I left the sails down.

The stillness was deceptive of the enormous powers at work to keep us here. I was at the complete and powerful whim of mother earth herself. Here, near the equator, the biggest, widest, part of her round belly, the force caused by her turning in space made air rise and move away, leaving me with nothing for my sails. A bit of wind might come with the northerly trades, but before it can cause a ripple it is met by its warm counterpart from the south, and, wrapped around each other like new lovers, the winds go nowhere but finally blend into one another, until each is unrecognizable from the other. Everything between them is detained in their embrace. It is an inconvenient love affair for sailors.

Stubbornly, even greedily, I wanted to wait and see what would happen. Under motor it would be easy to move the *Gracias* west and out of the doldrums. But I wanted to test my skills, my patience, and my ability to be in harmony with the will of nature. I neatly folded up my charts and went about my chores.

Watching the flat, calm ocean that morning, it struck me: nature is always content. It knows neither ego nor strife. Currents never race against each other to clock new records; nor do the stars push and prod, vying for a better position to display their brilliance. You do not see trees compete to reach the sky. Indeed, when a tree falls, its decaying leaves nourish the soil and feed its brethren. Nature is honorable. It doesn't fight nor plead or beg or cajole. It flows, it recedes, it shares, it allows. In the stillness, I tried to remember this.

In the afternoon I began my physical regimen. I didn't want to look like one of those scrawny, wind-beaten old sailors. At the Academy we had to do a hundred sit-ups and a hundred push-ups to pass our physical test. Since then, I never found the time to get to a regular training schedule. Today I had time. I got started, and quit when I had done fifty push-ups and sixty sit-ups.

The sea was still as calm and vast as an eternal swimming pool, and clear as glass. I could see schools of fish swimming two hundred feet below. I dove in and swam twenty yards off the starboard beam of the *Gracias*. I picked up the pace on the way back, putting in a sprint to challenge my speed and build conditioning. Back out I went, did the same, and in the end completed four "laps" this way.

I climbed back on board, the *Gracias* as steady as a dock on a lake. I lay facedown on her warm deck, resting my cheek on the back of my hands, stacked beneath my head. I enjoyed the feeling the sun on my back. It was hot here, on this bald face of mother earth, not a tree for shade nor a cool breeze. It felt like a luxury to stretch out and rest, unconcerned with the time or any schedule. I enjoyed the natural course of the day. Laying here, eye level with the deck, I saw a small pool of water from when I dripped aboard. I watched it slowly shrink into itself. The water returned to the sky, the salt stayed behind. A perfect exchange.

That moonless night I lay in my hammock and thought about my place in the world.

I was alone on this wide span of ocean. In the vast darkness, the sea reached from the *Gracias* uninterrupted in every direction, to the horizon, and again beyond that, and beyond that still. After many attempts in the past few days, casual at first, and later with some urgency, I hadn't been able to get a signal on the radio. I was too far from any land station, and if there were any passing ships, they were out of range. None of my friends or family knew my whereabouts. BJ likely pictured me halfway to Samoa by now. For a breath, my chest tightened at that thought. Yet in the next, the fear went away; I was free. A wash of relief went through me. Out of place from my original path through the South Pacific, I was untethered, disconnected from anyone's worries or concerns. Free from their expectations. No one was expecting me anywhere; I had no deadlines to meet. For the first time in my twenty-six years I was truly alone, with no one to be held accountable to, and no one to be responsible for. Just myself. It was just me, Captain Ken, single-handed, doing this all on my own.

I didn't feel alone. I was secure in the embrace of everything around me. The sea held us steady in her arms, lapping comfortingly against the *Gracias'* sturdy hull; my mammal and fish friends swarmed below; above, magnificent constellations showed me the way. It wasn't long ago that all men traveled with nothing but the stars as their guides, on land as well as sea. Faithfully following an invisible path marked by a mere spark of hydrogen and helium, trillions of miles away and already perished by the time its light reaches our eyes. It was a demonstration of faith that has proven itself true over hundreds of generations.

I looked at the constellations, each with their own story. Greek tragedies played out for me across this dark stage. It was better than any television program. As the sky became its darkest I spied the favorite of all Boy Scouts, the Big Dipper. Out of habit I counted all seven of its stars, and Polaris. A new shape slipped through the stage curtain of the horizon. There was Leo Minor, and to his right, the telltale zigzag of Lynx. The stars shone fine and clear, with no competition from man or the moon. It felt like each of them was within arm's reach. The longer I looked, the more

I saw of the lesser stars, they seemed to pop into the blank spaces between their bigger brothers.

The full Leo came next as this grand stage turned before me. Reliably, diligently charming, Leo the Lion had a reputation that preceded him. It was easy to be lured into his dark, vexing cave. Here he would lavish you with goblets of fine wine and plump the pillows behind your back, yet he always watched the entrance, waiting on another. His visitors soon realized they were captive bait; his true prey was the warrior who had come to rescue these naïve souls. To Leo's right I saw the faint lines of a long, upside-down letter "y." Cancer, the crab, was creeping forward from the corner where she lived.

Finally, here came the great, virulent Hydra, the main act of the evening. Like the showy, melodramatic star of a gaudy cabaret show, she made a slow, dramatic entrance, taking her time as she slid her long, serpentine body across the stage, waving her many heads across the sky. Nemesis of Hercules, Hydra was an evil, wretched beast who exhaled poison and had more heads than any man could count. When one was cut off, two more would grow in its place. Created by Hera, she was born for the purpose of bringing Hercules to his horrible demise. As he battles with her slithering form, trying to take off her many heads, the crab, Cancer, can be seen dancing around his feet, trying to distract him. In a harsh stomp, Hercules crushes her wide shell and returns the focus of his wrath onto that evil monster. Finally enlisting the help of his nephew, Hercules uses the ancient technique of cauterization to halt the growth of any new heads, and Hydra falls to her death. She, too, is cast about the stars, to keep an eye on Hercules, and the rest of us, for all eternity.

It was near midnight when I fell asleep. Hydra's entire form hadn't yet cleared the horizon, a task that takes her nearly six hours, with the slow pace and the good drama of a classical Italian opera. I knew there would be another showing tomorrow; I could catch the second half then. As I closed my eyes I was enveloped in peace and serenity. As transient and haphazard as it may appear, I had a sense of security about my place in the world. I was at ease here. I drifted off to sleep, utterly at home in my terrarium at sea.

CHAPTER TEN

Christmas Eve, 1957
Rome, Italy

We were a long way from home. The SS *Calvin* was docked in the busy port of Rome, halfway around the world. We'd had six days at anchor waiting for a berth. Poor weather had kept ships at dock and we waited out the storm outside the breakwater. After almost a week of tossing at our mooring, when we tied up and were granted shore leave the crew streamed off the ship as if it were afire. All but me. I lay in my bunk and faced the wall. I feigned a weak stomach. But the truth was I was feeling down. I missed home. I'd been gone for months now, and the distance was wearing on me. Maybe because it was Christmas Eve.

My first Christmas away from home I sent a telegram to my folks, full of punch and cheer. We were at the Port of Montevideo, Uruguay, for a four-night stay. I was enjoying my Sea Year. I learned what it was really like to live aboard a ship, an experience neither books nor the "Seamanship Lab" course back on campus could provide. The men on the SS *Alegra* were seasoned mariners, and tolerated myself and my classmate, Arnie Abrams, fairly enough. We were enjoying good weather in Montevideo. Wandering through the Old City near the dock we found a small restaurant that cooked huge, thick steaks on an open fire grill. Arnie and I made quick work of our small funds that week. We ate steak three nights in a row, and tried a fair share of *medio y medio*, a smooth blend of sparkling and white wines. Flowers bloomed in the parks, I was still excited for the adventures ahead, and as such it was just like the first day of summer. Hardly like a New England Christmas at all. In my joyful state I had the operator punch out this message: "Merry Xmas from Mont Urg All well."

A year later, much of my spirit was gone. I was in the Navy now, putting in my required active duty time after graduation, and I was counting the days until it was over. I was tired of the formality, the decorum, the strictness of it all. I wanted to get to work at sea where I could make some money. The sooner I got to work, the sooner I could build the savings that would launch "The Worldwide Tour." I lay awake at night in my rack daydreaming about it. To be able to go anywhere we pleased, with an unrushed, open itinerary. Rome in all her ancient, rocky majesty was just another port. Tomorrow would bring me a day closer to freedom. I wanted to sleep the rest of this one away.

There was a short knock at my door before it swung open.

"Hey, sailor, what are you doing? We're meeting in a quarter hour to go ashore. Get up! Smartly now!"

I feigned a salute from my bunk. It was Second Officer Flint Harper, Principal Jackson's nephew from Worcester. He too had come aboard the *Calvin* after graduating from Kings Point. He had decided to pursue a career as an officer, and had stayed on, slowly climbing the ranks. He had short, black curly hair and had started to grow a beard since we left New York. He had just trimmed it; the curls lay tamed and even across his face.

"I'm not going."

"What? Why?" His brown eyes got wide. "How can you stay on this vessel one minute longer? It's Rome! Don't you want to pay homage to the temperamental Neptune? And see the pretty Italian ladies? We're at liberty until 0600. After that, who knows when we'll be ashore again."

"Yeah, I know, I don't care."

"You still feeling sick?"

"I guess."

"Come on, it'll be a kick."

"I can stay aboard. Stop asking." The last thing I wanted to do was spend more time here. I was already ready to sail away, to finish my time with the *Calvin* and be released from the service. All I wanted was to be left alone in my bunk to sulk. Why couldn't the days pass quicker? Why did we have to stop in Rome anyway?

"Come on, Kenny. Just you and me then. You know what those old salts say, 'we may never pass this way again.'"

He was right. They did say that.

Here we were in one of the oldest civilizations of mankind. Where the myths of Neptune were born, in the country of Galileo's birth. That great man's contributions to navigation alone are far and beyond what any man would hope to accomplish in a lifetime. What kind of a fool was I to stow up in my bunk homesick like a baby in a place like this? My curiosity and yearning for adventure were roused. He had me.

Rome on Christmas Eve looked like a city touched by a magician's wand. Along every walkway, strung from pole to pole above us, little white lights glittered in the night, illuminating the arches and towers of beautiful, ancient buildings. It was like walking through a fairy tale. Most glorious was the Coliseum, lit along every edge and opening, as well as from within. It glowed like a majestic ship, grounded here for all to wonder about and delight in. The air on my face was clear and crisp, and I started to feel the mood of a New England Christmas.

A bus pulled up at the corner beside us, full of cheerful people who looked like they were on their way to a holiday party. I looked at Harper, he shrugged with a "Why not?" lift of his palms toward the sky. We hopped on.

We rode through the lit-up city. Streams of people moved along the sidewalks. Street vendors sold decorative wreaths, roasted nuts, and coffee. I saw a bent, elderly woman slowly picking her way through the throng. She had a train of half a dozen children behind her, each holding on to a long piece of rope tied around her waist, and following her through the crowds. After about ten minutes the bus came to a stop at the edge of a plaza. Everyone got off and we followed.

The plaza was an enormous circle, big enough to hold three football fields. Surrounding the plaza was an arcade featuring pillars that had to be forty feet tall. Hundreds of people milled about. In the center was a gigantic Christmas tree, twinkling with red-and-white lights. Along one side of the plaza a nativity scene was set up with life-sized characters and what looked like real goats and sheep. Everything here was on a grand scale. We stopped at a street-side stand for coffee.

"Ah, *Americanos!*" Seeing our uniforms, the boy, no more than fourteen, poured us each a small shot of espresso in a teacup and topped it off with hot water. It was rich and hot and better than any coffee we had tasted in months.

The church bell tolled; it was nearing midnight. I noticed people were starting to move toward the entrance of the large church at one end of the plaza.

"Eh, sailors! Get going!" The coffee seller was waving us over to collect his cups, and pointing toward the church. "It's time, go, go!" He motioned toward the crowd.

We fell in behind several families and soon were moving with the crowd into the church. As we passed through her palatial front doors I found the name of this magnificent building carved into the stone wall in square letters. Saint Peter's Basilica.

We entered a large passageway topped with a high arched ceiling. I smelled candles and incense. Tall white pillars lined the walk, along with carved statutes of ancient characters. The walls were trimmed in gold panels. The floor was tiled in beautiful white marble. There was a feeling of regality, that we were entering the home of a king.

The passage led to the great sanctuary of the church. Inside, there must have been a thousand candles. The warm glow made a cozy atmosphere. The crowd moved us along, Italian chatter and bits of laughter bouncing off the church walls. It was almost full and we found ourselves crowded into a pew near the back.

On the edge of my seat I looked around wide-eyed. I had only seen buildings like this in my history books. I couldn't believe how elaborate it was in person. The domed ceiling reached at least three stories high above the great sanctuary. Decorated in the ornate Roman style, scrolls of gold went up the walls to meet the fanciful designs in the ceiling. The grand dome peaked at the center of it all, smaller circles mimicking it as they fanned out across the ceiling. The windows alone were works of art. Majestic stained glass in rich reds and purples depicted figures that recalled the saints. They were aglow in the candlelight.

As the place warmed, we took off our coats and settled in to our tight space on the pew. We were two specks among this great scene of the faithful before us. Who were we to luck into this stately celebration? The pews behind us filled, and it was standing room only for the rest of the crowd. They filled the entire back hall and the atrium we had come through.

The crowd began to quiet, the silence moving in a quick wave from the front rows to us in the back. A man in white robes appeared at the front. Through a speaker system we heard him announce something in Italian, then something in Latin. When those around us bowed their heads, so did we.

With a final "Amen!" he came down the steps from the pulpit and stood aside. A group of men in black robes moved together in a pack past him toward the small stage. From within their assembly a man in white emerged. He climbed the steps and assumed the pulpit.

Elbows nudged, people whispered into each other's ears. Soft gasps of wonder went about the room.

"Il Papa!" they said. Pope Pius XII was at the altar.

He began his Christmas Eve Mass with some words in Italian, and soon switched to Latin. We followed with the movements of our fellow churchgoers. Standing, sitting, reciting, kneeling along with them. I will never know the full meaning of what he related there, but I will always remember the warmth of and beauty of the place. The beautiful glow of candlelight shimmering off the ancient gilded walls and colorful windows. The smiles of those around us, eager to hear Christmas Mass. The warm church held the collective joy of all those who cherished being in this divine place.

The Pope finished his Mass with a final declaration. Maybe he said it in English in deference to the many visitors there that night. But it was the one phrase I remembered: "May peace be with you!" The crowd rose, and as I stood I found myself in the embrace of the elderly Italian woman who had been sitting beside me. She was about the size of a ten-year-old, and I gently returned her hug, bent over to reach around her small frame. The small gold cross pinned to her collar caught my eye. It looked like something my mother would wear. I smiled at her and let go. I noticed the man in the pew before me had turned around and was reaching back for an embrace. Hugging all around seemed to be a Christmas tradition in this place, and we respectfully joined in. I even gave Harper a quick clasp before the members of our pew began to move, pushing us out of the church. Among the snatches of Italian I heard a voice call again, "may peace be with you!"

I carried this joyful sentiment in my heart as we made our way out with the crowds. It was 0200, and the night air had sunken into the plaza outside. Yet it was with a warm glow that we left that church, among the crowds of well-wishers and the faithful, dispersing into the night.

Harper was smiling. "That was neat."

"It was amazing! I never thought we'd see the Pope himself! And what a building! It's something we'd only see in the movies back home."

"Yeah, it was cool." Harper laughed. "And you wanted to stay aboard in your bunk tonight!"

I laughed too. Now it was a murky memory, too ridiculous to be true. I was glad we had taken our little adventure ashore, that we had been caught in that crowd at the plaza and gone along with what the night offered. We were a long way from little Leicester, Massachusetts, and, indeed, we might never pass this way again.

CHAPTER ELEVEN

April 7, 1962
Location: 9° 10' 18" N
                  148° 21' 30" W

The wind had been high for the past two days. Both sails were full, and the *Gracias* was hitting her stride, moving at a clip that brought back my racing days at Kings Point. I relished the spray on my face and the wash we left behind. If the *Gracias* could keep up this pace it would help make up some lost time.

We were day twelve out of the Marquesas, and according to my reckoning that morning, we were at 9.1N and 148.33W. This was still 521 nautical miles from Hawaii, maybe another five days sailing. If the wind held today again we'd make another hundred miles. It was a good pace, considering those doldrums days, and especially single-handed. I was at the helm from sunup to as long as I dared each evening. When the wind softened I reefed the sail and locked the tiller, content to move at a slower pace. It had to be done, in deference to the safety and well-being of the captain. There was always a time when I had to give in to the growling of my stomach.

The days of standing in the cockpit, moving at a nice speed, were delightful. As we moved forward at a healthy pace, the horizon approached and approached again. Each crest of wave marked another tiny fetch of sea we had crossed. It all looked the same, blue wave after blue wave. Some variations came in the clouds; they changed shape a bit as they moved across the sky, then a new batch appeared, going through the same formations as they passed. So we moved, across this great sea, and it felt as if we were standing in place. There were no landmarks to show the passage of miles. Indeed, the hands of my watch provided the only landmark. As they swung around its face I knew I was making progress. I came to realize that, while not always obvious to the eye, things were changing, all around me. My coordinates on board changed. The topography below changed. While invisible to me, the stars above had moved to a new vantage point from where they left off at dawn. I was witnessing the eternal movement of time and tide.

It got so I could tell the time of day within the hour by the changing colors in the sky. The pale, fair mornings made way to clear bold sunshine by 0700. Then the day was upon us. Sunny blue skies took over. They stayed bold until the sun was directly overhead. This caused a reprieve of sorts. Directly above the sun's rays seemed to whiten the sky, softening the day around. As the sun passed over my mast, the strong blue sky returned. When the daylight hours grew short, the sky relaxed into rich pastels once again. Peach and gold and pink streaks filled the horizon. The sun slinked down toward the sea, casting its silvery rays across the water and leaving shimmers on its dark blue face. By 1900 the last lingering light faded away.

LEFT AT HIVA OA

It was always a reward at sunset to bring my sextant on deck and chart my progress. Taking my bearings, I found that at the end of this day we had made a hundred and twelve miles. All to the good. I was thankful for four days of good wind and good travel. By my reading, we had moved east a bit; the tradeoff of the full sail. I would make this up tomorrow by being more conservative with my sail and tacking port until we were back on course.

After a hearty supper of potatoes and fish, I stepped out onto the aft deck with my harmonica. Tonight I was in a show tunes kind of mood. At Kings Point we made an annual cultural field trip to Broadway, a few busy miles and yet a world away from campus. In the long silent days at sea those famous songs played back in my head.

We boarded chartered buses, the whole class of us, and made our way through New York's city streets until we reached the theater district. There we clambered out, sneaking peeks up to the towering skyscrapers, before lining up on the sidewalk beneath the theater's awning. Through the crowds of people we would make our way inside. In our dress uniforms we stood out and often people made way for us, like we were firemen or police officers, headed to an emergency. But the only urgency here was to make a stop in the head before climbing upstairs to fill our rows in the balcony.

I liked sitting in the balcony. From this vantage point you could see the magnificent auditorium in its entirety. Fancy molding trimmed the arches over the doorways. Grand pillars gave a sense of strength and history. In some theaters, even the ceilings were decorated; patchworks of beautiful designs in gold and burgundy framed each of the light fixtures and fanned out to the far corners of the room where they met more molding trimming the edges of the ceiling.

Watching our fellow spectators was exciting too. We couldn't help notice the young ladies. Often, for a matinee show, they came with small groups of friends. They wore colorful dresses, fitted at the waist and with full skirts that fell well beneath the knee. If we happened to run into a group in the lobby they would look at us demurely; a collection of fawns with soft eyes that happened upon us bucks in the woods, wondering what our next move would be. The bravest among us would smile and nod and give a "how do you do?" and they would fold back into their small herd with smiles and giggles.

Evening shows were different. The girls didn't come in groups but were accompanied by young men in suits. They wore equally flattering gowns; these were longer and in more elegant grays or navy blues. In these cases, even the bravest of us never said "how do you do." For this reason, we preferred the matinees.

It was a whole new world for me, and the fact that we got to skip a day's worth of classes was great too. Some fellows would have preferred the movies but I loved the live music and dancing. *Guys and Dolls* was one of my favorite shows. I knew most of the score by ear. I also liked *My Fair Lady*.

The *Gracias* rolled lightly in the gentle night sea. I decided to make a go of a one-man show. I found my legs and stood on the rear deck, facing aft. My audience was in the sea; the house lights were down and it was pitch dark there, but for their eyes; little sparks of water lit by my night lantern. They sat rapt, awaiting my performance. I must begin.

"Ahem!" I cleared my throat, sticky with the first vocalization I'd made in days. "Good evening, ladies and gents. I would like to present you with a selection of songs from the Broadway hit *Guys and Dolls*." I put the harmonica to my lips and started with the lively "Bushel and a Peck." The audience seemed to be leaning forward in their seats, tapping their toes with the rhythm. Keeping the momentum, I ran right into "Sit Down, You're Rocking the Boat." I added a little jig as I played. In the most unprofessional fashion I had to chuckle to myself, causing me to miss a few notes. I think I heard a laugh or two from the audience as well. It was all in good fun. I played the lesser-known "If I Were a Bell," and, finally, I moved into the signature tune, "Luck be a Lady Tonight." I ended with a dramatic crescendo, holding that last note long and loud, and folding into a deep, humble bow. However, the audience had a lackluster response. All I heard were some gentle claps, as if the water lapped against the hull.

In the morning, it was the silence that woke me. Coming out on deck I feared what I would see. The sky was a pale gray; the horizon lost in the distance. The sea was calm again, laying like a smooth, gray bedsheet all around me. The wind had stopped, nary a current moved below us. I found a dim spot of sun and tried to take my bearings, and then tried again. Had we moved in the night? I must have miscalculated my readings yesterday. At my desk, I reviewed my charts. A trim line of small penciled x's marched across the Pacific, mostly in orderly fashion. The distance between each represented a day's travel. But now my pencil veered off the path and went south, to 7.5 N, 148.1 W. We were back in the depths of the doldrums. Elbows braced on the desk, I put my forehead in my hands and looked down at the charts. If this were correct, it was because by going full and by, leaving much of our course to the wind yesterday, we had pulled off to the east more than I predicted. Damn it. We were far into the dead seas. It would take a lot of motoring to get out of here and into the northbound current.

The amorous embrace of the conflicting winds that trapped us here was likely to be temporary. In a lover's quarrel one of the trades would turn its back to the other; its angry gusts would rise and fill my sails. If the spat grew, they easily could conceive a wriggling, screaming little squall of gusty wind and heavy rains that would push us forward.

Once again, I could wait for the wind. It might take a few days. I had no way of knowing. This meant the progress I'd made over the past four days would be wasted. Just when I was catching up, here I was set back again. What a waste of time and energy. My other option was to use my fuel to move out of here. If my calculations were correct, I was looking at a hundred miles of motoring to get back in the good current. More if they weren't.

I went to the forward storage compartment. There were two twenty-five-gallon gas cans there. I unscrewed each cap and peered in, just to be sure. They were both full. My fuel gauge showed the tank was half full. I had enough to make the distance under power. It would use most of my gas supply, but we would get across this piece, in two very long days. Was it worth it to make up some time?

I considered my options. If I chose to motor, I might end up burning up all of my fuel and still not making it across. Or should I extend my stay here at 7.5 N, 148.1 W, waiting for a wind that might not come? Another option was to stay in this doldrums stretch and let the *Gracias* drift north with it. We might miss our mark completely and drift pass the Hawaiian Islands, blindly on our way to California.

At least I had time to think about it before making a decision.

On deck I picked up the half dozen flying fish that found their deaths on the *Gracias* last night. These little morsels were no bigger than my hand, and they made a tasty meal. Tiny marvels of nature in their own right, they have long, lightweight pectoral fins that carry them over the water like dragonflies skimming along a lake. I cleaned them and pan-fried them, skin still on, seasoned only by saltwater. They were a convenient, easy meal, showing up on deck periodically as their flights above the water went astray.

After breakfast I made another weather check. The sky and water had changed from gray to bright blue. Still, no wind. I decided to wait it out a day, and see what tomorrow might bring. Decision made, I went into my doldrums schedule.

I started with my morning exercise routine. Intermittent sets of twelve push-ups and sit-ups. After ten sets of each I relished jumping in the cool, refreshing water. I swam off the beam, counting off twenty strokes, turned around and came back. With each stroke I reached far ahead, pulled my hand back through the deep thick water, and reached again with a new stroke. I kicked out my legs in a flutter behind me. It felt good to stretch and move this way, after standing at the helm for the last two days. I must have stayed in over an hour. I lost count of my strokes and found myself further and further from the *Gracias*. I was enjoying the feeling of moving under my own power, gliding along, creating my own current in the still sea.

Refreshed after my swim, I decided it was time to face the chaos below deck.

It's remarkable the mess that occurs on a small vessel when you spend long days at the helm. Everything below falls into quick disorder. There were dirty clothes kicked into the corners of my cabin. A stack of dishes filled the sink. The cushions on the salon benches were hanging on in disarray; several had toppled to the floor.

I filled a bucket with seawater, added a long dash of liquid dish soap, and gave it a stir. I placed my dirty clothes in there for a long soak. I took a bottle of bleach to the head and gave it a good scrub down. The galley was next. I washed the dishes and put them away neatly. In the salon I tucked away my books and charts, ensuring things were snuggly placed. Something rolled of the bookshelf and I put my hand out, catching a black plastic knob midair. It didn't have a nautical or mechanical look about it. I set it on the counter and continued my straightening. Later it dawned on me what this piece was: the regulator for the pressure cooker. It had blown off that day during that crazy broad's disastrous attempt at cooking beans. With the serendipitous mood of finding something I hadn't known was missing, I reunited it with its owner so I could make beans for my supper later.

Soon after dark I enjoyed a hot meal of beans and potatoes in my neatly appointed salon. The *Gracias* sure cleaned up good. Satisfied that my day had been a productive one after all, I went on deck to lay in my hammock and take in the evening stars.

My eyes traced out Ursa Major, the Great Bear. I remembered this story. A beautiful young woman caught the eye of Jupiter, the king of Gods. He followed her, watching her, waiting for a chance to be alone with her. This didn't go unnoticed by Jupiter's wary wife. To hinder his lustful desires, she turned the beautiful young woman into a bear. Lost, alone in the woods, this new bear wandered into the sights of a young hunter. She recognized him as her son, from the time she was human. As he took aim, the benevolent god Zeus, overseeing it all, quickly turned him too into a bear, and cast them both into the stars. Ursa Major and Ursa Minor, as mother and son, they would live together for all eternity.

The lustful desires of man can spur anger and jealousy, change the world, and in this case even the heavens. It was the ultimate intangible factor; impervious to the laws of physics, there was no way to control it or to predict it. Men are not alone in this; women are no better. Their dallying can wreck families and ignite a fury in a man's heart that changes lives and destinies. I had seen it myself.

It was still dark when I woke that November morning. I went to the small front room looking for one of my toy trucks. A light was on in the kitchen. I turned the corner and saw her standing at the stove, still in her coat. She bent to light a cigarette on the burner. After inhaling deeply, she turned and blew a stream of smoke across the kitchen. She saw me there in my pajamas.

"Hi, Kenny! Come over to your mama." She crouched down and I walked across the cold linoleum floor to her. She smiled and wrapped her arms around me, pulling me close. Her itchy wool coat smelled like the cold air outside. She kissed the top of my head, then stood, taking another deep drag on the cigarette.

"What are you doing up so early? You know this is the hour for madmen and the milkman!" She laughed. I didn't get the joke but I giggled anyway.

"Where are you going, Mama?"

"No place, Kenny, I'm home now." She kicked off her wobbly heels and took off her coat, draping it over a kitchen chair.

"Do you want to play with my trucks?"

"Sure, Kenny, let's play."

She set her cigarette in an ash tray and carried it into the living room. I pulled my toy truck from behind the sofa and pushed it toward her. Her eyes looked weary. Her lips were a pale pink, almost white, the red lipstick she usually wore wiped away. She yawned, squinting so her eyes became small slits for a moment, her mouth a big, pale oval. When she saw me watching her, she smiled and her face brightened.

"So, what kind of truck is this, Kenny?" She wheeled it along the floor with her hand.

"A dump truck! This one's a fire truck." I crawled back toward the sofa and pulled out the fire truck.

"Is there a fire?"

"Yes! At the post office! We have to hurry!"

"Let's get a move on then!" My mother followed close behind me, crawling across the floor in her dress and stocking feet, pushing the dump truck. We motored through town this way, putting out several fires and dumping things along the way.

I knew he was there before she did. I felt him filling the doorway. His face was dark, his eyes small. Was he mad because we were playing without him? But I knew he wasn't mad at me; just at her. His voice boomed through the room.

"Where have you been?"

My mother turned quickly toward him, still on the floor, one hand resting on the dump truck between us. She smiled up at him.

"Nowhere. Anyway, does it matter? I'm home now."

"Does it matter? You're my wife. You're supposed to be home all night. You have a son to take care of."

"I am taking care of him! Don't you see us playing here? Kenny's fine, aren't you, Kenny?"

She smiled at me and poked at my belly.

"No, he's not fine," my father answered for me. "He needs his mother. How can he be fine when she's stumbling in at dawn like a tramp?"

A tramp? What was that? An animal? I knew cats crept around in the early hours.

My mother looked down at the floor. I saw tears pooling in her tired eyes. It couldn't be a cat, she loved cats. She caught me looking and our eyes locked.

Her eyes were green, but not just one color of green. They changed. When she laughed they were bright, like the sun shining through summer leaves. When she was angry they flared with gold and brown, like dried grass. Now they were dark like a pine tree, and full of sadness.

"Marty, how can you say that?" She pushed herself up from the floor and stepped over to him. Leaning into his shoulder, she put her arm around his waist. "I was just out for a walk."

He pushed her away. She stepped back, teetered for a moment.

"Cut the crap. You can't fool me, Helen. Where've you been all night?"

"I told you, I was taking a walk. I couldn't sleep."

"A walk? Sure. Probably down to the pub. Which one was it this time? The Moose Lodge? Or did you go over to Finnegan's? Spend your evening clowning around with the other drunks? Just tell me so I know what to expect when the guys at work start talking."

"I'm not a drunk."

"Well, whatever you are, you're my wife. And it's breakfast time. Get in the kitchen and get to it. Your son is hungry." He lifted his chin toward me. "If you don't give a damn about me, at least think of him." He turned from the doorway and disappeared down the hall. My mother glanced at me, then went to the kitchen. I followed. She put on her coat and stepped into her shoes. She saw me there as she turned for the front door.

"Where you going, Mama?"

She didn't answer, but when she came close I saw her eyes were lit with that golden-brown.

"I'll see you later, Kenny." She bent and gave me a kiss on the top of the head. She left the smell of cigarette smoke and the click of her heels behind her as she moved across the room. In the open doorway the pink sky of early dawn briefly framed her small shape. The door closed behind her. I didn't see her again.

As the mother bear and her son moved higher in the sky I tried to temper the tears rising in me. How could she have never come back? Didn't she care about me? Was it true what they had said about her? My sadness turned to anger. She was the sort of wild woman not to be trusted. No wonder my father never spoke of her. It was probably better for all of us that she had moved to Florida.

My peaceful reverie under the stars ruined, I went to my cabin and tried to escape into sleep.

The rodeo raged around me. I heard buzzers going off, the fans cheering, and a brass band in the distance. I couldn't find my boots. I had looked in my truck and dug around in the trailer. Where were they? I was next, I needed them right now, or I'd have to go in my stocking feet. A whistle blew—it was time to get lined up at the chute. I had a tough horse. He was reputed to be the meanest bronco on the circuit. I cringed at the thought of him—why had I pulled his number? Climbing up on the rails, my feet slipped on the smooth metal pipe. Well, I didn't need boots to ride a horse anyway. Another whistle blew. It was time. Balanced across the top of the chute, I looked down at the horse below me. He was all muscle and he snorted and stamped his hooves in the enclosure. And he was green. He was the green of a summer elm, bright and cheerful. How did this horse turn green? He couldn't be as tough as they claimed, with that pretty green. My body pitched sideways. Was he bucking already? I wasn't even on. And again. I fell off the railing, hitting my shoulder on the way down. The horse took off, dirt flying from beneath his hooves as he darted into the arena. I hit my shoulder again. And finally woke to find myself deep in my berth, rocking heavily side to side across my bunk. The *Gracias* was rolling in heavy seas.

I crossed the salon quickly, headed for the companionway to go on deck. My foot slipped out from under me and I fell hard onto the mess floor. I had slipped in a pile of beans. Everything was put away snug and secure the night before, but I had left the pressure cooker, full of beans, on the counter to cool. Now it was on the floor, a stream of the slippery suckers running away from it across the floor, every which way with the toss of the boat. I put the pressure cooker in the sink and quickly cleaned up what I could with a few swipes of a towel. Damn those beans.

On deck I stood for a minute, getting my balance and rubbing my eyes. The wind was up, and we were rolling hard from port to starboard. There was no moon, and clouds had come over us, hiding the stars. It was very dark. Based more on what I couldn't see than what I could, I determined a squall was on its way.

The feel of the wind teased my cheeks. I wanted to catch it. We had sat all day in the doldrums. But where were we? Which direction should we head? How severe was the weather coming? In a forty-foot boat my options were few. We could stay here, sails down, bailing water as needed, and ride it out with the hope of not losing our position, nor damaging the *Gracias,* or myself, for that matter. Or I could raise the sails and capture the wind, giving the *Gracias* the best chance at staying above water, and the opportunity to move out of the doldrums. I went below deck for my foul-weather gear.

My compass reading showed the storm was coming from the south-southeast. While it was the perfect direction to sail downwind and toward Hawaii, I'd have to rig my sails so they wouldn't tear in the strong wind. I'd use the jib sheet to keep us steady. But first we would have to turn around. I got about it.

Here upon me was the moment I imagined, a troubling vision lingering at the back of my mind since leaving Hiva Oa: Single-handedly rigging and raising sails in the face of a storm. Gusts continued to heave the *Gracias* and I had to move smartly. The danger involved with riding the squall came to mind. I pictured waves pouring over the bow, swamping the *Gracias* and pushing her down into the depths of the sea, me along with her. Or the sail could pull the mast over, tipping the *Gracias* on her side and knocking the lot of us into the water. I saw myself tossed about in the stormy sea, my last moments filled with terror and misery. But those thoughts quickly passed. Crossing the Pacific alone was an all-or-nothing gambit, from the moment I made my decision to sail. It had to be. This was merely one phase of the journey. In my mind, I quickly mapped out each task I had to complete. I didn't have time to be scared. It was time to focus, to use my training, to make the best of these cards I'd been dealt.

I calmly went through each task. I tightened the boom vang, ensuring it would keep the boom down in full sail. Then I moved to the helm, where I gave a slow, strong turn to the rudder. Rising and falling over each crest of wave the *Gracias* slowly turned. I held my breath as she went abeam of the current. Making our way around that final corner I exhaled and she came to line up her stern directly toward the prevailing wind, like a horse turning its rump to the rain. I moved to the mast and heaved on the long line of the mainsail. Up it flew, and unfurled completely, giving a sharp slap in the wind. The *Gracias* plunged forward. Too much sail. Fighting the strong wind I slowly cranked it down, turned the boom slightly abeam and we moved forward again, still bouncy, but better. I let up the jib sheet, and our passage became smoother.

Back at the helm I held her direction straight into the oncoming waves. By my estimate they were close to fifteen feet high. We rose up the front of each one and came down the back, sometimes landing hard. This jolting vertical motion was hard on my legs and would slow our progress, but there was no way around it. The wind continued to push us, filling the sails, and I hoped to maintain this delicate balance as we moved forward. If the wind switched I would have to jibe, turning the sails around, and we could lose our forward direction. Or capsize.

Moving faster across the sky the rain clouds caught up to us. There was a smack on the back of my slicker, one on my hood. Many more came. It was a rain of fat, heavy drops, and I feared for a downpour. I saw distant flashes of lightning out of the corner of my eye. I started to count the seconds after the flash. In the rushing wind I couldn't hear any thunder. I had no way of knowing the storm's distance. But the wind pushed it along quickly. The rain continued for a few minutes, then eased as the clouds blew over, and we carried on.

The mast light above had blown out, and only the bow lantern cast a single bright light into the dark waves before us. Each wave was a copy of the previous one, an endless flow of bumps to ride over. I couldn't see beyond them to judge the sea ahead. There was only the rise of the black wave in view, then the trough, then the rise again. We went on this way for hours, moving almost blindly in the dark.

Even with these conditions I was happy to be sailing. I automatically went through the motions to keep us moving forward, hoping that when the sun rose and I took my sights, we would be closer to our destination and not further away.

CHAPTER TWELVE

July, 1961
Chilean Sea

The Navy took BJ and I in separate directions after graduation. But we had a plan. Once we completed our service, we would set to work and save our money; between the two of us we could find a suitable sailboat and be able to fund our supplies. "The Worldwide Tour" would begin. When my active duty commitment was complete, I went to work in the best place I knew to earn money and not have to spend a dime—I joined up with the freighter *SS Alamar*.

As second officer, my duties included safety of the ship, the cargo, and the crew. This included the assignment of medical officer. I had taken a series of first aid courses at Kings Point, but I wasn't prepared for the realities of caring for dozens of crew members at sea. Here, men faced all types of maladies. Diarrhea was one of the most common complaints. This could be caused by the unusual foods we ate in new ports or spoiled provisions. I learned to ask about their symptoms, as there was a chance they may have something serious, like the flu, malaria, poisoning, or even intestinal worms. Learning the intricacies of the men's digestion systems and what seemed to set them off was a time-consuming study during my first weeks on board. In most cases, rest with a dose of bismuth helped settle things down. With contagious conditions, we sought to isolate the patient as soon as possible. God have mercy on the ship's medic that had an outbreak of the flu spread through his ship.

I was on the bridge reviewing charts with the first mate when the radio crackled and I heard my name. "Bohlin, you're needed in the sick bay. Over."

"Roger. Over."

I hastened from the bridge and down the nearest ladder to the third deck and down the gray passageway to the medic's office. The small space, usually closed off and empty, was always cold. As I approached the bay I saw the door stood open, and stepping over the threshold I found the room full with men. At the center was one of the *Alamar's* engineers. I didn't know him, but identified him by his blue work coveralls, smeared with grease and other stains. He was fresh from the engine room. As I got near I saw a streak of blood on his right arm.

He held his hands before him at chest height, almost in prayer. The left was clamped down over the right.

Two other engineers and their commanding officer were crowded around him. The heat of the engine room came off of them in the cold bay. I looked at the chief engineer for an explanation.

"Cassidy's severed his finger," he said gravely. A knot tightened in my stomach and the tension crept through my chest; my palms were warm and damp. A severed finger?

I looked into the man's face, still and pale as a morning pond. His eyes were wide and he sat with his back straight and tense.

"Are you OK, sailor?"

"Yes, sir. Just worried about that finger." I was too.

"Let's have a look." I nodded at his hands, one still clutching the other.

Slowly, he removed the greasy, bloody rag that was clamped over the injured finger. Beneath, I saw his thick index finger, the fleshy tip cut off with a deep gash. The fingernail on the back was intact, the cuticle lined in dirt. The front was a bloody divot. It looked alien and unnatural, a bite the size of a chestnut taken out of the tip. Blood leaked down the finger and across his palm in a slow trickle.

Many strange maladies and conditions can occur at sea, and here was one before me. A detached fingertip. I was no surgeon; I was twenty-five-years-old and had taken a few first aid classes. Who was I to fix this man's finger? I looked into his wide blue eyes. I knew he was worried about more than the finger; he didn't want to end up a disabled engineer peeling potatoes in the galley. I recalled the very first rule of first aid training I had learned in Boy Scouts: "Stay calm." This didn't just refer to me; I realized I needed ease my patient's fears as well. I took a deep breath.

"And the other piece?" I didn't know what to call it.

"Right here, sir." One of his mates held another greasy rag toward me, bunched around the fingertip, I presumed.

"We're going to need some ice."

One of them went for ice; I found some alcohol swabs and set about cleaning the wound.

When I was done I put a thick pad of cotton over the finger and asked Cassidy to hold his hand aloft, above his heart. I put the bunched-up greasy rag on the desk, my back to Cassidy, and unfolded it gently. In the center lay the flesh of this man's fingertip. It was as real as if it had still been on his hand; the lines of his fingerprint were outlined in grease. My stomach churned. I took a deep breath. I regarded it again, in my mind considering that it was just another component of this man. Like fixing a machine that had lost a part, I had to put this back in its place. Using a pair of forceps to hold it still, I set about cleaning it as I had the rest of his finger.

"Do you think there's a chance you can save it?" Cassidy tried to look around my shoulder from his seat on the exam table, a mix of worry and hope on his face.

"Well, I don't see why we shouldn't try." I turned toward him. "I've heard it's possible." He relaxed a bit, letting out a long breath and slumping slightly on the examination bench.

The engineer returned with a small bag of ice. With him was Davis, our chief petty officer. He stopped at the desk, the room already full. "I heard what happened, Bohlin. What do you aim to do?"

We were off the coast of Chile, along the maze of hundreds of uninhabited islets and twisting fjords where Chile and Argentina begin to merge, approaching Fin del Mundo, as they call it, "the end of the world." We were scheduled to dock at Ushuaia the next morning.

"We need to get on the radio. We might find another medic nearby who can give us some advice. Let's put the tip on ice for now."

The engineer held the bag open for me, and, using the forceps for only the second time in my life, I picked up the bit of flesh and tenderly put it in the ice. He gave the bag a spin, twisting the top closed, and tied it off in a knot.

At the corner of the desk was a small radio; Davis got on it and searched for contact, either at sea or on land. After a few minutes we heard a response, from a Chilean fishing ship, the *Buena Suerte,* fifteen nautical miles to the south of us.

"This is the SS *Alamar,*" he announced, "at fifty-five degrees and six minutes latitude south, seventy-two degrees and forty minutes longitude west, moving approximately fifteen to eighteen knots, destination Ushuaia. We have a medical emergency. Seeking a medic's assistance. Do you have a doctor on board? Over."

"*Que? Una emergencia de medico?*"

"*Si, si, tengo un doctor?*" Davis replied in his broken Spanish.

"Oh, *si,* yes, sir, *si,* we have a doctor on board."

We heard a garbled comment in Spanish outside of the radio. The operator was calling over his shoulder to his crewmates.

"May we speak with him? It's an emergency."

"*Si, si!* Hang on, we go to find him."

"OK. Bien." Davis put down the handset. "They have a doctor onboard. If he only speaks Spanish, we might be in trouble."

I looked at the chief engineer. "Any of your guys speak Spanish? What about Cruz?"

"Rafael? He's from New York."

"Yeah, I know. But he's Spanish. Puerto Rican, I think. Haven't you had that stew he makes?"

"Stew? No, Bohlin, I haven't."

"You should try it sometime."

"Yeah, I think he speaks Spanish." It was one of Cassidy's mates. "He's off duty, I'll go find him."

"All right, thank you." He left, giving us a little space in the small room.

Soon the radio crackled again and we heard the operator's voice.

"*Alamar?* Come in. Over."

"Si, we're here. Over."

"Yes, OK, *el doctor esta aqui.* Over."

"OK. *Gracias.* Over."

The radio crackled again and a deep, booming voice came over the airwaves.

"*Hola, Alamar. Este es Dr. Vela. Cual es su emergencia de medico?* Over."

"Hello, Dr. Vela. Do you speak English? Over."

"No, *no se.* Over."

"OK. *Tengo un* translator, *uno momento.* Over," Davis said in a mix of bad Spanish and English.

Rafael entered the bay with a heavy step over the doorframe. He had a sleepy look on his round face, and was wearing an undershirt and plain dungarees. His curly black hair held a bit of white lint in it.

"Ay, Cassidy! What happened, my friend? How did you do this?" He became wide awake, pressing into the crowd and looking over a shoulder to see Cassidy's hand, still held above his heart with a piece of cotton clamped over the index finger.

"Changing a lightbulb." Cassidy looked down.

"What?"

"Those lights in the passageway? One had blown out. When I went to change it, I dropped the cover. I heard it break, but when I went to pick it up I didn't know I was grabbing the broken end."

I knew the lights he was talking about. The clear glass covers were thick, forged in some long-ago glassworks that believed in quality. A broken edge would be as sharp and thick as a hunting knife.

"Oh no!" He looked at his friend, worry across his chubby face. "What are you going to do?"

"Mr. Bohlin is going to see if he can sew it back."

"What? Gosh, I hope he can." He looked at me.

"Cruz, we need your help." I looked at him directly. "We have a Dr. Vela on the radio, but he only speaks Spanish. Can you translate for us?"

"Me? Wow, I don't know. It's been so long since I was home. I can try, sir. I will try," he said with more conviction. He muttered in Spanish, "*Oh mi Dios!*"

"See, there you are, that sounded fine to me!" I said.

He looked up from the floor, eyes big in his round face. "OK, yes, sir."

He moved next to Davis at the desk.

"Hello, *Buena Suerte*, do you copy? Over," Davis inquired.

"Yes, *sí*. Over," the doctor said.

Rafael took the radio. "*Hola, Dr. Vela. Soy el marinero Cruz. Copy?*"

"*Yes. Cual es su caso de urgencia? Over.*"

"*Ay…perdio su dedo. La punta fue cortada, completamente!*" I saw a thin stream of sweat trickle down the side of Cruz's face.

Dr. Vela's calm voice conveyed no shock over the injury. He asked Cruz another question in Spanish.

"He wants to know, how is his hand, the finger that's still there?" asked Cruz.

"It is good, healthy, it was a clean cut," I replied.

Cruz relayed this in Spanish.

And so it went. Dr. Vela's deep voice came through the radio with very clear, precise instructions. First, he had me give Cassidy a local anesthesia. He explained how to find the vein in his upper arm, and I forced myself to keep my eyes open as I made the injection. While I waited for it to set in, I cleaned the finger and the fleshy tip again. The skin around the cut was white and clear, and the bleeding had stopped. Next Dr. Vela instructed me to put the pieces together. I set the severed tip in the hole of his finger. It fit there easily, just like an egg in an egg carton. Now I had to apply a thin line of surgical tape around the circumference of the wound. When I had my needle and sutures ready, I was to remove the tape from a small section, make stitches along the exposed length of skin, stop, remove more tape, and proceed for the next length. It seemed like a simple enough procedure. Dr. Vela ensured me it would be easy.

"It's no different than sewing a bellboy back on a shirt," Cruz relayed, wiping the sweat off his forehead with his forearm.

All heads turned to him.

"*Botón*! Button! Sorry!"

So I proceeded, imagining it was not human flesh my needle went through, but instead maybe a sail that had lost some stitching in its hem. I tried to make the stitches small and orderly, like those my mother sewed on her quilts. One by one I went around the face of Cassidy's finger. Sweat built on my temples in the cold room. Finally, I had completed the circle. I tied off the suture like I was knotting a fishing line, wiped the flesh one more time with an alcohol swab, and wrapped it all in a thick bandage of cotton pad and tape.

We were lucky indeed to have found the *Buena Suerte* with Dr. Vela on board. When the surgery was complete, all of us in that crowded sick bay could breathe regularly again. Cruz thanked Dr. Vela profusely on behalf of all of us. We learned he was a traveling medic on his way to the South Pole to join up with an expedition there with the National Geographic Society. Luckier still was Cassidy.

By now four years had passed since graduation. I had faithfully sent most of my paychecks home to my father, who deposited them in the Worcester Five Cents Savings

Bank. I had enough to pay the balance due on my schooner. It was time.

I sent BJ a short ship-to-ship telegram.

"You ready?"

Late in the day I got one back.

"Yes, sir!"

The next day I put together my formal request to leave the United States. This had to be submitted to the commandant of my Naval District for approval, as I was still an ensign in the Navy Reserves. I set about typing up a formal memo on the clerk's typewriter. The young, slight seaman from Kentucky stood by, hands clasped behind his back, while I went about it with my usual hen-pecking style.

After a few painful minutes he interrupted me with a polite Southern "Sir?" I looked over. "Would you like me to do that? It might be…um…I reckon it would be a little more efficient that way."

"That would be splendid." I pulled the ruined sheet off the roller and moved out of the chair.

He rolled a fresh piece of paper into the typewriter and pushed his wire-rimmed glasses back with a finger. "OK, go ahead," he said, gentle as a grandmother.

"Ref: Bupers Manual Article H-31401." His fingers flew across the keys with a rich, speedy, clackity-clack that belied his soft country demeanor.

"OK."

"Number one. In accordance with reference (a) I hereby request permission to leave the United States for a period of approximately three years."

"Yes, sir." He was almost done before the words were out of my mouth.

"Number Two. The purpose of this trip is to, in company with a friend and his wife, sail the forty-foot schooner *Gracias* around the world."

The clacking stopped abruptly, and he looked at me. "Is that right, sir?"

"Is there a problem with that? Should I reword it?"

"Oh, no, sir. I was just surprised. I figured you for a career officer. You know, coming out of Kings Point and all."

I laughed. "Well, this sounded like more fun.

"OK, number three. Our approximate itinerary is as follows: Approximate ETD this area 1 September, thence to the East Coast to join the *Gracias*. We will then leave the United States and sail to the Panama Canal via the Caribbean Sea. Thence across the South Pacific via the Society Islands, American Samoa, the Fiji Islands and to New Zealand and Australia."

His fingers never slowed.

"You're getting all this?"

He stopped when my dictation stopped. "Oh yes, sir. Do go on."

"Thence across the Indian Ocean to South Africa and from there across the South Atlantic to South America and the Caribbean to the Panama Canal. Thence up the coast of Latin America to Long Beach, California, USA. Approximate ETA Long Beach, September, 1964."

The clacking stopped again. "That's quite an itinerary, sir!"

I grinned. "Isn't it great?"

We finished up with the formalities and I sent it off in the ship's mail.

Three weeks later I received a reply, forwarded from the *Alamar's* home port office in Long Beach. It was a standard form with the appropriate boxes checked. I especially loved reading this section: "You are hereby granted permission to leave the continental limits of the United States as follows." In the box below, where it said

"Countries to be Visited" was typed simply: "Trip around the world." I read it over and over. "Trip around the world." Finally, our time had come. Excited, I went to send BJ another telegram.

CHAPTER THIRTEEN

April 9, 1962
Location: 10° 07' 46" N
              149° 09' 52" W

As morning came the seas calmed, but the wind stood strong. I was happy with my decision to keep the *Gracias* moving the night before. She had done well through the squall; I was proud of my little schooner. In the quieter waters I locked her tiller and took a moment to take a reading. We had moved northwest after all, and made over a hundred nautical miles in the night. We were back in the right current and if the wind held today we would make good time again. I made note of the squall in my logbook and marked our current location on my chart, proud of our progress. We had moved a whole half an inch across the map. I adjusted my sails to take better advantage of the wind. The *Gracias* leaned into it, steady and willing as if she hadn't already put in a full night's work. I let her be while I went below for some breakfast.

I boiled a large pot of water for coffee; it had been a long night. While it brewed I cut off a chunk of salted pork.

In the hanging net above the counter I found a few tangerines. Still good, all these days away from their mother tree in the Marquesas. I took one up on deck with my coffee. After so many meals of fish and canned foods, its flavor was a sweet shock to my tongue. I relished the soft flesh in my mouth as sticky juice leaked down my chin. I threw the peel overboard and took a look at the day ahead.

The wind had calmed to ten to fifteen knots, with occasional gusts, remnants from the squall. That suited me fine. The clothes I had set about washing the day before still hung clipped to the rail, washed again with saltwater splashed up from the sea. Maybe they would dry today.

I brought a new lightbulb from the storage compartment below. I aimed to climb the mainmast to replace the burned-out bulb in the lantern. At the base of the mast I assembled my bosun chair, pulleys, and winches. Attaching the clips to the line, I pulled down hard, making sure it was locked. Next I put my legs through the various straps of the chair, pulled the seat up under my rear end, and buckled the waist strap. I leaned against it softly for a moment, and then let my full weight fall. All seemed secure. I clipped my satchel of tools to the line around my waist. Time to go up.

Hand over hand, I worked the pulleys and pulled myself up. The wheels were small, and even as I gave the line a good long crank I only moved a few inches with each pull. I swung side to side as the *Gracias* rocked in the gusts. In my mind I heard the voice of my old coach, Lieutenant Rainy, saying, "What are you thinking, Bohlin?" He had a point. Normally, one wouldn't climb the mast moving out at five knots for a minor errand like replacing a bulb. I didn't want to stop the *Gracias'* progress; we were still making good time on the last winds of last night's squall. I told myself it was a safety issue with the bulb. I would hate to think that we would be run over and smashed to smithereens by the next big freighter in the night who failed to see us due to the mere burnout of a bulb. Anyway, I wanted a look at the view.

With one hand on the mast to reduce my sway, I took a look from fifty feet above deck. The horizon looked even further away from this vantage point. The water there took on a silvery-blue hue, matching the color of the sky. In every direction the sea stretched far and wide, as plain as a perfect hay field. It was no wonder men once believed the world to be flat. That is how it looks. It was a brave sailor who went forth anyway, and found that the sea kept flowing at him, never ending. Many moons later, when he arrived back in his home port without crossing his own path, he began to realize he never needed to fear falling off the edge of the Earth; the world could not be flat after all.

I pulled a Phillips screwdriver from my tool belt and began unscrewing the latch to the lightbulb cover just above me. The screw loosened, and fell before I was ready to pull it free. I caught it midair, as easily as a juggler's ball, and placed it between my lips for safekeeping.

I exchanged the bulbs, replaced the cover and latch, and made it secure with the screw. I put the screwdriver in my tool belt and tucked the spent bulb in the waistband of my shorts.

I looked down the mast at the *Gracias* toward her deck. I admired her trim lines and perfect, balanced shape against the water, here a deep indigo blue. I looked forward again at the ever-elusive horizon. As we moved toward her it felt like she moved as well, backing away from us, like a recluse avoiding our visit. I stayed up there a while, taking in the sights, and wishing I'd brought my binoculars. Next time. I didn't want to push my luck. It was time to ease down. I could feel the wind had shifted some, I should get to reefing.

As I unlocked the pulley, a sudden gust pitched the *Gracias* portside forty-five degrees and I swung out over the water, sliding in a freefall on the loose line. The rope rushed through the pulley as I dropped. One hand still held the failing line, the other tried to get a grip on the mast, tilted at an angle above me. My hand grappled and banged along the length of it as I slid, hitting hardware and ropes and unable to get a hold. My feet swung out to knock into the sail. For a quick moment I calculated the risks—was it better to plunge into the water than to land on the hard deck below? But if I became separated from the *Gracias,* in these winds she'd sail away without me. Then, as suddenly as the first pitch, the *Gracias* righted herself. I swung hard into the mast, hitting it squarely with my torso, bouncing away, then back. My legs quickly wrapped around the mast and I clung there, useless rope still in one hand, catching my breath. I looked down. I had slid down the entire mast's length; my feet hung just a yard above the deck.

I slowly let myself down. Stupid, stupid mistake. I touched my shoulder. It hurt like hell. What was I thinking? All could have been lost in that stupid decision.

As I went below deck my body began to stiffen and ache. I set about examining the damage. I took out the used bulb and pulled down the waistband of my shorts. On the front of my left hip I found a perfectly round red mark, like I'd been hit with a baseball. Next I wanted to look at my shoulder. It hurt to raise my hands over my head. I began to shake as I pulled off my T-shirt. The fear from the fall remained with me; I was anxious and my head spun with worries. What if I'd dislocated my shoulder? I consulted the little five-by-seven-inch mirror hanging in the head, turning it upward to see my torso. There was an egg-shaped bump on my collarbone. A long red mark ran from the top of my left shoulder down my chest. It was six inches wide, matching the width of the mast. It began to darken to purple as I watched.

I took two aspirins and a long drink of water and eased down onto the salon bench. I moved my shoulder in a slow, small circle. It felt like it was on fire. But it moved; it was still in its rightful place.

I was out here alone. I couldn't take stupid risks. No one would save me. If I'd broken a bone when I made contact with the mast I'd be in bad shape. If I fell off the *Gracias* in high winds I'd be doomed. I needed to be careful and steadfast in using all precautions. I took a deep breath and tried to reassure myself. I was OK. I was still aboard. I hurt, but they were only bruises. It could have been a lot worse.

At sunset I checked my sights. We had made another sixty nautical miles. I logged my notes for the day, grimacing as I described my senseless safety error, and I penciled our new location on the chart. Little by little, we were making headway. We were fourteen days out of the Marquesas Islands. I thought we would be able to see at least a hint of the islands ahead by now. Birds and driftwood were often clues that you were within a few days of land. I hadn't seen a thing.

Along with the ache in my chest and hip, an ominous feeling settled in my belly.

CHAPTER FOURTEEN

September, 1961
Annapolis, Maryland

"Ahoy, Captain! Come above deck for inspection! Smartly now!"

I smiled in the galley. I was glad to hear that voice; BJ and Jean were here. I climbed up on deck and saw them waving from the pier.

"Ahoy yourself, sailor! Good to see you. Have a pleasant drive?"

BJ laughed. They had come almost five thousand miles, driving from Long Beach to Annapolis. "Let's just say I'd rather be at the helm of this beauty. Hot dog! She looks great, Ken. Permission to come aboard?"

"Granted!"

They stepped aboard and I gave BJ a quick hug. Jean came over and I gave her a kiss on the cheek. Since graduation, BJ and I had traveled to nineteen countries between the two of us. Somehow he had also found time to come stateside and get married to Jean, his longtime girl. She was beaming with excitement.

"She looks marvelous, Ken. Will you give us a tour?" Jean asked.

"Why of course!" I made a gallant sweep with my hand and indicated they go ahead of me toward the stern. Since I had made the initial deposit, BJ and I agreed that I would pay off the boat in full, while he and Jean contributed to our fuel and supply costs. This made me "captain," by default. It wasn't a title I would ever hold above them; we were all equal crew in my mind.

I found the *Gracias* the previous January when I had a four-day port stay in Baltimore. I took a bus to the Annapolis marina, known as "America's Sailing Capital," to take a look around. A "For Sale" sign was hanging askew on the chain at her gangway. I liked what I saw beyond the chain. No one about, I stepped over it and made a closer inspection. She had a fine shape, and while worn in places, she seemed sound. The companionway hatch was unlocked so I let myself in. At the bottom of the steps, glancing right, I saw the galley; tucked into the corner on the left was a small counter and seat, used as a navigation desk. An old-style ship-to-shore radio sat there, cobwebs joining it to the desk. She had a teak interior, and green-and-blue plaid-covered benches, with little curtains made to match. Years ago, this sailboat had been someone's pride and joy. Today everything was covered in dust. I went to the front of the boat to inspect the forward cabin. Tarps were draped around the room. Peering under them I found three bunks lining the walls. The aft cabin had a full bed, sheets tossed aside like it had been slept in last night. Except for the layer of dust covering it all.

I learned she had been for sale for a while, and the owner was willing to take a deposit and let me pay off the balance upon possession. He lived in New York City and hadn't spent much time with her lately. He called her the *Gracias*. Sailors' superstition says it is bad luck to change the name of a boat. The *Gracias* suited me fine.

When I came back in mid-September I gave her a more thorough inspection, including the engine room and storage lockers. I found old gear that had to be thrown away. Behind the ratted ropes and rusted varnish buckets was a layer of old dirt and rat droppings. Since I had the compartments open and empty, I decided I may as well clean them too. I spent many days on my hands and knees, face deep in a locker, scrubbing every corner with bleach and water. I wanted her to be "spic-and-span," like our boats at Kings Point.

In the galley was the worst mess; here there was grease splatter on the backsplash behind the stove, up the wall, on the very ceiling! The *Gracias* began to smell like laundry day at my mother's house as I went over almost every interior surface with bleach. But it seemed to work the best, and it was cheap. Between the greasy galley and the cache of empty purple cloth Crown Royal bags I found tucked on a closet shelf in the rear cabin, if I were to hazard a guess I would say the previous owner was a bachelor. If he wasn't, I'm sure his wife wished he were.

It was September 25th. We were already behind the schedule I had set, but such are things related to the sea and human beings. I had hoped to set sail on September 20th. When BJ wrote to tell me they were driving, not flying, I knew we'd be set back some. That was OK, there was plenty to do to get the *Gracias* ready while I waited for them. I still needed to do some repairs to one of the sails and I needed BJ to help me with the rigging.

Over the next several days we cleaned, oiled the woodwork, and did other duties to prepare for the voyage.

It was great to have their company. I knew BJ would work hard and we were a good team. We had crewed side-by-side on many boats at Kings Point. Our biggest adventure so far had been the Bermuda Race, a six-hundred-mile sail from Newport, Rhode Island, to Hamilton Harbor, Bermuda. It was an honor to be picked for the ten-man crew representing Kings Point. Our first long sail as midshipmen, we enjoyed the five-day voyage with the Mariner's team, where we slept in shifts, and rotated through our deck duties. We finished a respectable forty-third of eighty-nine boats in the race that year. Staying a few days in Bermuda after the race was a kick too. It gave us a taste for life onboard in a tropical port.

Jean was a spirited girl with a cheery disposition and the willingness to work. It was a comfort to know we had a nurse on board. She wasn't much in the galley but BJ and I had a lot of mess meal experience and we shared our ideas with her. She was sharp and caught on quickly.

Their third night aboard I came out of my cabin and found her at the tiny galley sink, washing her hands before dinner. She seemed to stay there, scrubbing, for an inordinate amount of time. "How's it going there?" I asked, pointedly looking at the sink. "Lady Macbeth?"

She laughed. "I know, Ken, sorry to use so much water, I just can't get my hands clean." She held them up, black with the all the brass cleaning she had done that afternoon.

"Here's something that will help." I got out the gallon of bleach from under counter in the head, and poured a bit into a cup, adding a few drops of dish soap, and giving it a quick swirl to mix. "Rub this in and let it soak for a minute, should come off after that."

"Thanks, Ken." She took the cup from me. "She's starting to look pretty good, don't you think?"

Indeed, the *Gracias* was sparkling with the effort Jean put in. And BJ loved spending time oiling the teak interior; it seemed to soothe his disappointment that the decks were merely fiberglass.

We taught Jean the different knots we used onboard for the rigging, and many other neat things sailors can do with rope. She began making a hanging net basket to stow our gear. We also taught her how to make a "baggy wrinkle," first unraveling lengths of rope and then weaving the strands together in long lengths. These were hung from the rigging to make neat cushions to protect the sails from rubbing against each other. We even had our own Baggy Wrinkle Contest, giving Jean an award for Best Beginner Baggie Wrinkle, but mine took first place, hands down. It was almost a shame that we were going to put them to work.

On October 3rd we were ready. The *Gracias* was ship-shape in every way. Supplies were loaded and neatly stored. I finished the paperwork for leaving Annapolis and we were cleared to sail.

"You're ready to get the heck outta Dodge, aren't you, Ken?" BJ had found me on deck, standing at the helm in my foul-weather gear. An early fall rain had come upon Annapolis. He knew I was antsy. It was my way to take my time in preparation, but once I was ready to go, I lost all patience. I had crossed that line two days ago. This weather was holding us up.

"You know it, BJ. According to the reports, this should clear tonight. If it's fair in the morning we'll head out. It's time for us to go, past time. I just hate to leave under a dark moon."

BJ didn't dismiss my worry as an old wives' tale. Not for a journey like this.

"It can't be helped; we can't wait another two weeks. But the tide will be high in the morning, and if we leave before noon, that ought to help some." Those were always good omens for the start of an expedition. He continued, egging on my excitement. "It's finally here, can you believe it? 'The Worldwide Tour' is about to begin!"

"It's what we always wanted BJ, and now we're going to do it. Who knows what adventures lay before us?"

"I can't wait to find out."

In the morning, just a few clouds danced across the bright, sparkling blue sky, freshly cleansed by the rain. A light wind came from the east.

I left the harbor master's office with a quick slip out the door and moved swiftly up the pier. It was all I could do not to run. I was like a kid with a key to the candy store in his pocket. I passed other fellows on boats docked alongside, easily going about their regular chores, scrubbing decks and mending sails. None of them were about to set sail this very morning on a journey around the world! Poor fools. I gave brief waves and "good mornings!" and tried to maintain a cool demeanor as I hurried back to the *Gracias*.

Jean and BJ were waiting on deck.

"You hardy sailors ready for the adventure of a lifetime?"

Jean had a broad grin. "Yes, sir!"

BJ gave me a little salute. "Ready and able, Captain!"

"Let's shove off!"

It was a beautiful fall day in Maryland. As we motored across Annapolis Harbor, the three of us stood at the helm, beaming with big smiles in the sunny morning. We were like children at Christmas. We looked forward to feeling that way every day as we circumnavigated the world; a new horizon before us at every dawn. The breeze stirred the elms that lined the shore, the rush of red-and-orange autumn leaves seemed to cheer on our departure. The wind on our faces beckoned us toward the sea.

"Ready, mate?" I looked at BJ.

"Ready, Captain!" He stepped to the mainmast, where he untied the mainsail and began to pull on the halyard. The sail rose and unfurled before us, full and bright with the morning wind and sunshine. We were off.

Our route was to take us south through the Eastern Intracoastal Waterway. This was an easy, smooth passage for the beginning of our journey. We wouldn't see the open ocean for 1,500 miles, when we reached Florida.

Fifty miles out of Annapolis we entered Chesapeake Bay. The water was rougher than we expected. Although I had never been through the Bay, I had read much about it. It seemed that it was a peaceful, calm body. But another fall thunderstorm was brewing, and the wind picked up the water, and the *Gracias*. We pitched and heaved in the foul weather all day, doing our best to keep her moving forward, and to keep ourselves vertical.

That night, sails down, we gathered in the salon. The *Gracias* pitched so much Jean could barely keep the chili pot on the stove. We scarfed down what we could, and I went up on deck for my watch.

The fresh air helped settle my stomach. Rarely did I get sick on board but tonight was beginning to feel like an exception. The water on the bay was gray, like no other I'd seen before; the *Gracias* rolled and pitched in the howling wind. Clouds crowded around us, and a mist began to spread across the bay, dark and imposing, reducing visibility to about fifty yards. We had our bow and mast lights on; it was best to sit tight and hope not to be run into by another vessel.

BJ came up the companionway and without a word went straight to the rail. I left him to his business. After he straightened up, I called out, "OK, buddy?"

"Now I am. I just couldn't keep that fine dinner down."

"I know the feeling. I'm holding on as best I can myself."

The words were just out of my mouth when Jean came up the ladder, zipping past BJ and finding a place at the rail herself. She had hardly finished when saliva filled my mouth and then my stomach clenched. I ran to the rail. There went the chili.

We hung on through the night, taking turns on deck and sharing a can of ginger ale to settle our stomachs. By morning the wind had moved on and the sun was trying to peek through the clouds. I went to the galley and set about making a pot of coffee. Near the stove the wall was dripping; wet streaks ran down it, disappearing behind the counter. Not damage to the *Gracias* already, so early in our voyage! I looked closer, and found sometime in the night water had pushed through an unsecured porthole, and had leaked down the wall and in to the compartment below that held our canned goods. It was halfway flooded. Labels floated in the water; bare, silver cans shimmered below. Besides a haggard crew, it was the only harm done from the storm. The current still churned, and we set about raising the sails and moving out of that rough, angry bay.

I was balancing a tray of freshly cleaned and seasoned striped bass as I climbed up the ladder, headed for the grill on deck, when I heard a fierce splash in the water. A moment later it was followed by another. I set my tray down and headed toward the bow.

"Ken! Come in! The water's fine!" BJ was in the green-gray water, waving at me off the port bow. Jean swam up to him.

"It's quite lovely, Ken!" We were a day past our difficult passage through the Chesapeake Bay, anchored at Virginia Beach for the night. A swim sounded like a great idea.

"Coming!" I pulled off my shirt and jumped overboard in a tight cannonball, making a thick splash and sending me down deep. I popped back up to the surface. The water was refreshing indeed. I swam over to BJ and Jean.

We treaded water there, feeling the coolness on our skin. It was that slim time between day and evening, and the *Gracias* sat dark. Across the water was the faint outline of forest along the nearest shore. The sun had disappeared behind it, leaving only silhouettes against a pale pink sky. Birds collected there, singing their evening songs and finding their nests for the night.

"Tell me, fellows, how is it that being *in* the water feels so much better than being *on* it, some days?"

"Doesn't it, though?" BJ agreed.

"Well, there's a theory about that," I said. "It's called the Contradiction of Paradox Theory. We learned about it at Kings Point."

"Oh? What's that?" Jean asked.

"Remember Carney's class, BJ? He talked about it. How it feels like crap to be in rough seas when you're on board, but so much better when you're actually *in* the water."

"Oh yeah. It was first hypothesized by that one guy... what was his name?"

"I forget his name. But the theory proves true. I believe we've experienced it right now."

"Really, well, that's interesting," Jean said.

"Isn't it?" BJ agreed.

"Yes. We had a similar theory in nursing school."

"Really?" BJ looked at me, and back at Jean. "What was that?"

"It was called the 'Bogus Sham' theory, otherwise known as B.S.!" She leaned back in the water and kicked her legs in our direction, splashing water on our faces. BJ had himself a smart lady.

The darkness settled around us and we swam over to the *Gracias* in the quiet evening water. It was time to fire up the grill and cook that fish.

We had fair sailing down the rest of the waterway. On October 14th we made Ft. Lauderdale. To celebrate this milestone we decided to take a few days of R & R. It felt good to be ashore. We went out for our meals and took long walks on the beach. We enjoyed hot showers at the yacht harbor club house.

Grocery shopping was no longer a tedious chore but instead it was like a trip to the fair. In the supermarket everything looked bright and new. The deep-red slabs of meat behind the butcher glass almost glowed. Fresh vegetables made our mouths water. The smell of bread baking was tantalizing. After many days of fish and canned goods, it was hard not to pick up everything in sight. On my way back to the harbor I bought a twenty-pound bag of perfect round oranges from a street vendor. It was a lot, but I hoped they would enhance our meals. We had made a rule onboard for all those cans missing labels: whatever you opened, you had to eat. More than once I'd seen Jean's disappointed look when she was hoping for clam chowder and instead got a can of creamed corn. A fresh orange might cheer her up on those occasions.

"No scurvy aboard this vessel!" I announced as I placed the bag on deck.

BJ took the twenty-pound bag of ice from my other hand. "No sir! And I can't wait to grill up those steaks tonight."

From here we set our course for Colon, a major port in Panama and the eastern entry of the Panama Canal. To get there, we would sail through the Bahamas, making our way west, past Cuba and the Yucatan Peninsula, and then along the coasts of the Central American countries of British Honduras, Nicaragua, and Costa Rica.

It felt good to take the *Gracias* out on the open ocean for the first time. She seemed to enjoy the journey as well. Her sails filled, we glided through the water, gently bouncing over the crests of current. BJ enjoyed being at her helm, and easily adapted to her sails and rigging. When the wind held we moved out smoothly, and all was well. When it was slack we had problems.

Our second day out winds lagged and her pace slowed to about four knots. The *Gracias* lost her smooth forward motion, and picked up a little hitch in her roll. BJ got sick that night, unable to hold down his dinner. But unlike the time at Chesapeake Bay, he was the only one. Jean and I were fine. The next day the winds stayed the same, and BJ suffered again. Jean dug around in the bin of cans to find one still with its label, and heated up some chicken noodle soup. He couldn't keep that down either.

"I don't know, Ken. It can't be food poisoning. I've only had soup since Ft. Lauderdale. You two are OK." He took a long pull on his cigarette. We were standing at the bow, enjoying the fresh breeze at our moderate pace.

"Maybe you picked up a flu bug back there."

"That's what Jean thinks."

"Drink lots of water."

"She's been on me about that too."

I knew he was miserable. It was no fun to feel sick on board, whatever your ailment. It is tough when you can't escape to solid ground. He was stuck here.

I had learned a lot during my medic days on the *Alamar*, and now again I consulted my volume of *The Ship's Medicine Chest and Guide to First Aid at Sea*. I ruled out food poisoning, and he didn't seem to have any other symptoms that might accompany a virus. I couldn't put it together.

We decided to take a rest in the tranquil waters of Key West. While it was another delay to the journey, I hoped it would give BJ a chance to get over his sickness.

Anchored here, protected by reefs all around, the *Gracias* hardly rolled beneath our feet. As far as you could see, the sea ran out shallow and clear over a sandy bottom. It shone in a translucent, tropical blue that glittered like crystal.

Each day we took the skiff out to a nearby reef to fish and dive. BJ dropped a line overboard and I took my spear and dove in to the warm water. All the delights of tropical waters were here. Nestled in the sand, barely visible in its buff tones and roughly textured shell, I found a starfish as big as my head. The reef fish streamed by in beautiful flashes of yellow and purple. Of these I only recognized the parrot fish, easily identified with its beak-like mouth. It had a blend of blue-and-peach-colored scales, and seemed to change colors depending on which way you looked at it. I found it hard to kill any of these beauties, and kept my spear by my side only for protection in the case of an aggressive shark or ray.

BJ did far better, hunting with the anonymity of the fishing line; he pulled in several, pink, big-mouthed hogfish. They were delicious on the grill.

After a week of sunny days and swimming in calm waters we felt rejuvenated. It was BJ, now, who was getting antsy. "I'm fine, Ken. We need to get a move-on. I know you wanted to give me a break, and thanks, it's been great, but we have to keep this baby moving. You know we're in the middle of hurricane season. Anyone who lingers around here this time of year is a dummy. What did Max used to say? 'Bunny?' Don't be a bunny, Ken. Let's get going while the going is good."

"You're right, we're pushing our luck every day we stay. You sure?"

"Yes, sir. Let's get a move-on." We planned to pull anchor in the morning.

CHAPTER FIFTEEN

October, 1961
Florida Keys

Gray skies and brisk gusts greeted us at dawn. Clouds moved quickly above, flowing across the dull sky, seemingly in tandem with the swells pushing across the sea of the same grim color. According to the reports on the radio, bad weather was brewing to the south. I decided to set sail anyway. It was time to make some headway. If a storm was coming I wanted to get past Cuba and toward the protective coastline of the Yucatan Peninsula.

We made 120 miles our first day, working the sails and tacking into the gusts. We had closed some of the distance I had wanted to make, but the shoreline was still out of sight. Over dinner we listened to the weather report again. The storm winds to the south had increased, and it was now a full-fledged, Category 5 hurricane. They were calling her Hurricane Hattie. She had turned westward, and was forecasted to be heading right for Belize City. It was going to be disastrous.

After dinner BJ took the evening watch, and I sat below and reviewed my charts, mapping our course with the projected path of Hattie. What I saw stunned me. I went up on deck to smoke a cigarette.

"How's it look, Ken?" Jean asked.

"We're lucky we're up here. If we hadn't stopped in Key West, we'd be in the midst of her now." I looked at BJ. "Thanks for making us take a pit stop, buddy."

"Glad I could help. We sure missed a big one."

"We did." We stood there crowded on the aft deck, looking out at the dark choppy water in wonder. While we'd weathered rough seas before, none of us had experienced a hurricane. The *Gracias* might have been washed up on the rocky shore of a desolate Central American coastline right this moment, with the three of us long lost to the sea. We were lucky indeed.

The next day we made the Peninsula and began working south along the coast. The radio was busy with talk from other boats. There were hourly reports on the damage done by Hattie. Throughout Belize City buildings had been toppled. The power was out and the streets were flooded. There were warnings of all types of debris washed to sea in muddied rainwater, clouding the water and polluting the ocean for miles.

Most alarming were the calls for missing boats. A nearby US Navy ship coordinated the search. On their frequency we heard a constant stream of calls for missing vessels and their captains. There was never a response.

When the last light left the day behind, the sea became a different world. The cheerful blue water was replaced by a solemn blackness. Sky and water were the same, merged at the horizon into complete darkness, like being in an earthy cellar in the deepest night of winter. It was a quiet time.

During the late watch I let my mind wander. Looking out at nothing at all, I struggled to make sense of our position here, to place us somewhere familiar. This wasn't a New England pasture; there was no sweet smell of grass, nor the sound of wind through the trees. It wasn't a dry, wide desert; contrarily, we were afloat on a mass of water. We weren't on a mountaintop, raised close to the stars; no, we hung in the middle, balanced at the zero measurement of heights and depths. It felt like we could be in outer space; before us were millions of stars, seeming close enough to reach out and touch. I tried to relate to something I knew, to understand the wonder of where we were, but my thoughts always drifted and faded away, leaving my mind bare like an empty room. Then I would notice the smell of the salty air, and feel the gentle crests of the current, my hand still on the tiller, keeping the *Gracias* moving straight through the night. There my thoughts began again, lighting gently on what I saw before me, trying again to place us, before they moved on and faded like mist. And so went my shifts on the late watch.

I smelled coffee brewing. BJ was up.

A few minutes later, he came on deck, a mug in his hand. We were still in the deep pitch of night, the promise of dawn only in our imaginations.

"Good morning, sunshine."

"Hey." He rubbed a hand over his eyes.

"Sleep good?"

"Yep."

He sat down on a locker and took a sip from the mug. His watch started now, at 4:00 a.m. I stayed at my post. I knew it would be a few minutes before the coffee kicked in. He took another sip. Then a big yawn.

"Whatever happened, I slept through it all." He said this every morning, forgetting in his drowsy state that he was giving me the perfect setup. On cue, I began.

"You did! You missed the parade of submarines. They came out of the east and motored right alongside us for twenty minutes. I counted at least twelve periscopes, there may have been more. I think they were Commies. I swear I smelled sauerkraut when they passed."

"Really?"

"I kid you not! I think they're headed for DC."

"Ha ha," he said flatly. Another sip of coffee. Two more and he'd be alert enough for his watch. "Yeah, sorry I missed that. Did they glow in the dark too?"

"No, dark as can be. And quiet. They tried to just slip by." Yesterday I told him about the flying saucer and mysterious light display that lit up the sky at 3:00 a.m. "But I heard the dripping from the scopes coming up out of the water. That's how I spotted them."

"I see, said the blind man." There he was, setting me up again.

"No, you don't, said the deaf!" I quipped. I laughed at my own joke, partly out of habit and partly with tired delirium.

Now the sky was hinting at dawn with that barely discernible light of this hour, faint and ubiquitous; hard to tell from where it came. But soon the sun's rays would be blatant as they began to clear the horizon. My aim was always to get to bed before their brightness kept me from sleep.

BJ took a long sip from the mug and slowly stood. "I'm sure you're ready for a nap."

"I am indeed. Your turn, skipper."

He set the empty mug on the deck, made a long, dramatic stretch skyward, and stepped alongside me to take my place at the helm.

I went down the companionway, leaving BJ humming a slow, drowsy, version of "Blue Suede Shoes," behind me.

I was just pulling BJ's leg about the Commie submarines. But I had a feeling our Navy ships had been in these waters ahead of Hattie on another mission. They were keeping an eye on Castro and his bunch.

BJ raised an eyebrow when I told him this. We stared at each other for a moment. The Bay of Pigs attack on Cuba happened six months ago. Over a thousand men were said to be captured and held in Castro's prisons. Was something big about to happen here again? We were on leave from the reserves. We had our paperwork in order. This meant we were just ordinary yachtsmen, out for a sail. We both knew it was best to keep to ourselves and carry on. But it wasn't only up to us.

Two days after Hattie made landfall we were along the coastline of Honduras. It was a cloudy, quiet night. The stars were hidden and there was no moon. Jean and I were on deck, letting BJ have a rest below. As it was dark and the wind low we had dropped all but the foresail and were barely moving forward. We watched our progress as we passed small villages on shore. I could see a soft flicker of fire here and there, at times groups of bright lanterns. I imagined women cooking over open fires as they prepared beans and rice, and rich seafood stews made with coconut milk. I could almost smell it from where I sat.

Then, like the burst of a firecracker, the night lit up. The shoreline disappeared and the entire body of the *Gracias* was illuminated from above. The water around us had an eerie yellow glow.

Jean gave a start and a little shriek. I knew immediately what it was and my pulse quickened. Turning to face the source of the light I saw we were directly abeam of a 500-foot Navy cruiser, not twenty yards away. Alongside the *Gracias* she looked huge and menacing, like a great gray fortress holding a company of ready warriors. The ship had silently crept up close to us for observation. Shielding my eyes to the bright, shocking light with my hand, I looked up the side of her hull to the rail high above, searching for a crew member or watchman. I made out no one; there was nobody to call out to or acknowledge our presence. Then a voice came from above:

"Ahoy! Prepare to be boarded."

Boarded? Why? We were no military vessel. Soon a skiff was motoring across the short passage between us. They tied up aft. We had no choice but to obey their commands.

"Permission to come aboard?"

"Granted," I said, begrudgingly. We didn't want any part of this military operation.

The first mate came aboard and greeted me at the helm. He was in his mid-forties, with a brisk demeanor and alert eyes. His uniform and close-cropped hair were a stark contrast to my swim trunks and white undershirt. My eyes went to the service pistol at his waist. We were unarmed.

"Officer Mitchell." He introduced himself. "Are you the captain of this vessel?"

I met his salute with one of my own and answered. "Yes, Captain Bohlin, commanding officer, and ensign in the Naval Reserves. How can I help you?"

"You an Annapolis man?" he asked, studying my face and noting my young appearance. I wasn't old enough to have climbed through the ranks.

"Kings Point Merchant Marine Academy, sir."

He shook his head. "One of those. OK, here's what we're going to do." He was all business now that he knew we were merely reservists through the Merchant Marines and hadn't "paid our dues" like he and his enlisted men had. He beckoned to his second mate, who had accompanied him across.

"Percy's going to do an inspection. Just a formality." He gave a flat smile. "We can't be too careful down here. You have your paperwork in order?"

I went below for the paperwork and almost tripped over BJ on the steps. He'd been sitting there listening in his boxer shorts.

"Get some clothes on, mate, inspection time!" I playfully slapped him on the shoulder and went to my desk.

"What do they want?" he demanded. "Do we look like a threat? What a bunch of bozos," he added under his breath.

"We look like two Mariners who swamped his C.O. in the Bermuda Race. He's been hearing about Kings Point men for years and now's his chance to tell his own story about us."

"Ha! What a jerk." BJ went to the forward cabin for his dungarees.

When he was dressed we went on deck. I handed Mitchell our papers. He read through them carefully while Percy let himself below. There were two things they should be looking for—arms and stowaways. We had neither.

"Where are you three headed?"

"Panama, sir." I decided to keep my answers short.

"What for?"

"Coconuts, sir."

I felt BJ stifle a laugh behind me.

Mitchell looked at me sideways. "Coconuts?"

"Can't get any good ones stateside, sir."

He gave me a hard look, like I was a dummy not to be bothered with, and went back to the paperwork. "Yeah, OK." He flipped through the sheaf of papers. "Who's Bruce?"

"Me, sir." BJ stepped forward. He knew for all my feistiness these guys could put us in a jam if they wanted to. While our papers were in order, even the suspicion of some subversive activity could give them cause to stop the *Gracias,* detain us, even end our travel plans.

"You in the reserves too?"

"Yes, sir."

"Kings Point?"

"Yes, sir."

Mitchell lifted his chin toward Jean.

"And who's she?"

"My wife, sir." Jean gave a small wave at Mitchell.

Percy came on deck. "Nothing, sir."

"All right, boys, you're free to proceed. Be careful in these waters. Commies everywhere." He gave a stiff nod and he and Percy returned to their skiff.

The monstrous ship silently backed away from us in the dark, moving astern until we were in her bow lights. Then those were switched off and she went about her covert mission, like a shark slipping away into the water in search of new prey.

"What was that about?" Jean said.

"Just those Navy fools. They're going nuts over these communists. I'm glad I'm not on active duty right now," BJ replied.

"I can't believe they allow that," Jean said.

"It's common practice. Stupid but common," BJ said.

The darkness had come back. The warm fires ashore drifted behind us now. We continued in the soft wind, thankful for the dark and the quiet. Jean went to bed. BJ and I stayed up, still steaming about our visitors.

"What were they thinking? Sneaking up on us like that! As if the three of us are any kind of threat."

I laughed. "I know! That was one for the books. We should do a write-up and send it to someone at Kings Point. They could use it for a case study." Military missions and maritime safety didn't always go hand-in-hand. Our instructors had given us many examples of this. "And besides that, how dare they endanger us leisurely pleasure boaters?" I said this part in jest; now we were the ones with the freedom to enjoy the sea. Those poor brutes aboard worked long days and spent months away from home. BJ gave a short laugh, and then said solemnly, "I guess times are tense; you never know what you're going to run into down here."

"I bet the Canal will be loaded with GIs too."

He nodded. We were both familiar with transport and staging activities; these were a major part of Merchant Marine responsibilities.

"I'm going to hit the hay."

"OK, see you in a few hours."

As the quiet night settled around me a thousand thoughts ran through my head. Were the communists as serious as we feared? What did Navy intelligence know? Would we soon be in the midst of a third world war? Would Castro be the next Hitler? Were the Russians involved? Would BJ and I be called back into service? How did things look on the other end of the Canal?

It had to be better there. What did they care about Commies in the Galapagos anyway? In Tahiti, Tonga, and Samoa, they couldn't be concerned about the affairs of these crazy men. I was anxious to move out of the testy waters of the Caribbean Sea and make our way to the calm, peaceful Pacific.

CHAPTER SIXTEEN

November, 1961
Colon, Panama

The winds continued to be light and we traveled at a three to four knot pace. I was confident we would reach Panama in another seven to ten days. However, I was worried about my first mate. BJ's sick spell had returned. His thick, strong frame had slimmed over the past weeks. I was out of ideas to help him feel better. Even Jean, a nurse, was confused.

"Ken, I don't know what's happening with Bruce. I know he doesn't want to tell you this, but he's really in bad shape. He took his watch OK yesterday, but he was so weak afterward he laid down to take a nap and didn't get up for six hours. I'm worried about him."

I leaned back from the helm and tapped the ash off my cigarette over the rail.

"I noticed. I'm not surprised. If he can't keep anything down, he's got no fuel to work with. What do you think is causing it? A strange tropical bug? He doesn't seem to have any of the symptoms of a virus, as far as I can tell."

"Well, of course, he wouldn't want me to say this." She looked into my eyes. Hers were damp and full of worry. "In my opinion, he's seasick."

"Seasick? BJ? What?" I laughed.

"You know, he's never been sick like this before. But I noticed it started around our second week, when the winds slowed a bit."

"Yes, that's right."

"Well, when we were going faster, the *Gracias* had a much smoother pitch to her. I think when things slow down she has a different motion. And I don't think it agrees with BJ's stomach."

It was true you always had to get used to a new boat. Being in accord with your vessel was something that came over time, as you worked and slept onboard, and eventually you became in tune with her, so much so that you could place every step in anticipation of her motion. They were all different, based on their sizes and shapes. The little S-Boats we raced at Kings Point were so tiny they moved underfoot. The Navy frigates we worked on only pitched in heavy seas. If you never adjusted to your ship, your stomach would surely suffer from the movements. In any case, Jean was his wife and had him under watch for the past several weeks. She would know.

"Well, I suppose it could be." I hesitated. "But what does that mean? I don't think there's anything we can do to make her feel any different, or run more smoothly. Unless the wind picks up. And even then." I didn't want to say what I was thinking.

"I know," She looked down at the deck. "I don't think it can be fixed."

The harbor at Colon was along a wide, flat expanse of land trimmed with low green mountains. Houses painted in colorful Caribbean pinks and blues stood in rows lining the outlying areas. We could smell grass, flowers, and the earth itself as we got closer to land. Nearing the harbor we saw the taller buildings of downtown. The waterfront was very active. There were vessels of all kinds, including large freighters, Navy cruisers, smaller fishing boats, and yachts and sailboats of all classes.

We pulled into port near sunset. The harbor master's office was closed. They had strict regulations for yachtsmen here. It was easy to cross in the big freighters we worked on. The paperwork was handled quickly and you were given your crossing time within a matter of days. For those who were using the canal for mere pleasure, we had to wait up to three weeks for a crossing. As everything at the marina was shut down for the day, only the boats' owners were allowed on shore. I took the skiff over and did some shopping for us.

It felt good to stretch my legs as I moved along the sidewalk. I passed by many street vendors, selling grilled meat, and fresh mangos chilled in ice. They were tempting, but I had something else in mind. I rounded a corner and looked up the block to the next street. Yes, there it was, the same small market I shopped at last year when we stopped here on the *Alamar*. The front door cut across the corner, on the diagonal. A wooden sign hung above it. "*Almacen de Ezequiel*."

A low counter lined the wall directly to the right of the door. Behind the counter the wall was stacked with colorful cartons of cigarettes. We may as well have been in a souk in Istanbul, for the variety he had there. Parliaments, Pall Mall, Marlboro, Camels, Wind, Cosmos, Gauloises, and more, ready to satisfy the habits of any traveler who came through the door. Further along the wall were shelves of booze, all kinds here too. A small, hunchbacked man in a pink, short-sleeved shirt stood halfway along the length of the wall, taking rum bottles out of a box.

"*Hola, Ezequiel! Como estas?*"

"Eh?" He placed a last bottle on the shelf and pivoted toward me. "Oh, sailor Ken! How long since I've seen you!" he replied in English. He looked me up and down, over the top of his glasses. "What brings you down here? Did you come to spy on Castro? That's all we hear about over here nowadays."

"It's been crazy, has it?"

"Oh yeah. They've been bringing shiploads of boys over here, getting ready for what, I don't know. Good business for me, though. What are you doing down here in Colon? You working another ship?"

"Don't you remember I told you I'd be back one day? I'm on my way around the world."

"Well, good for you, sailor Ken! You worked hard for those people, saved your money, now you can do what you like. Just in time, too, I think."

"I think so. You still have that delicious meat you marinade?"

"Oh yes, in the back cooler."

I moved through the narrow aisles, hung with signs in both Spanish and English. In the back cooler I found the meat, cut into thin strips and marinating in a tangy red sauce. I also picked up a case of cold beer. I knew they would appreciate that. Next to the cooler case was a freezer. Through the clear top I saw round plastic buckets. Ice cream? Here in Panama? This was a new item for Ezequiel's shop. I slid the lid open to pull out a bucket, and my eye caught a cardboard box filled with red bags in the corner. Frozen strawberries. I got them too.

I took my load of cold items up to the counter. It was all I could carry; I'd have to make a second trip for ice.

"You still smoke those Kents?" the old man had a hand on a carton on the shelf behind him.

"You remembered! Yeah, give me one of those."

"How could I forget? Sailor Ken, smoking his Kent cigarettes!" He laughed.

"Do you by any chance carry any Alka-Seltzer?"

"This port already making you sick?" He fished among a bevy of pigeonholes in the wall to his left, and finding the box, placed it on the counter.

"No, Ezequiel, my first mate's not feeling so good."

"I hope this helps him, that's no good."

We had a fine party there on the deck of the *Gracias* that night. We grilled the meat, cooked some rice on the stove, and finished it all with ice cream topped with half-thawed strawberries. BJ felt better in port, and even indulged in a beer.

The American presence was heavy at this port in Colon. Anchored with a fair-sized army base, there was a medical center and a PX, a YMCA, and an active baseball league that included locals, army guys, and the ex-pats who were "passing through," albeit for an entire baseball season. It was a comfortable place for Americans. It was cheap to live here, and still on the dollar. Panama attracted the soft-handed adventurers; those who wanted to live aboard their vessels and go abroad, while keeping the conveniences of their homeland. It was very clean and pretty compared to what I had seen in ports in Africa or the feisty Colombia immediately to the south. But they were a friendly bunch and free flowing with their gin martinis, so I kept those thoughts to myself.

We made fast friends with our neighbors. There was a couple from Maine with their teenage sons aboard the schooner on our portside; on the other was a wizened brown-skinned whip of an older man, who introduced himself only as "Woody," in a twangy voice, a cigarette tucked in the corner of his mouth. He had a thick bunch of hair, graying at the temples and pushed up into a curly flop on top of his head. We called him "Woody Guthrie" among ourselves.

It was almost Christmas. Many boats were strung with sparkly lights up their masts and around the rigging. Our neighbors from Maine had a Christmas tree on their forward deck, made from cut palm fronds stuck in a coffee can. It was a festive time, and we were invited to a different party on a different yacht almost every night.

BJ began gaining back his thick build after a few weeks in port. I realized Jean's theory was probably right. He wouldn't be able to sail the world, not on the *Gracias*. As much as I had come to love her, I would have traded her for any other boat in that moment. Why did I pick her to begin with? And how could something as simple as the shape of her hull and the depth of her keel make such an impact on our voyage? I couldn't understand how things could have come to this. It wasn't fair. BJ and I had planned this for years. He had wanted it even more than I did. He was full of remorse.

"I'm sorry to let you down, buddy. I wish I could do it; I just don't know if I'm going to feel better at sea. I can't be the crewman you need. It wouldn't be fair to you."

"Don't say that, BJ. You're the best crew a guy could ask for. I'm sorry I picked a ship that disagrees with you. Of all the boats I could have bought! It never crossed my mind. Especially with a sailor like you. I never thought this could happen."

"Me neither. Hey, don't let the word get out, OK?" He looked at me sideways and laughed. I laughed too. "The *Gracias* is a fine little yacht; she'll take good care of you.

You just need the right stomach for her." He laughed again. I would miss this guy.

BJ and Jean inquired around the docks about a passage back to Long Beach. They found space on a freighter headed that way. For "The Tour" to end like this was heartbreaking. How would I continue on without BJ and Jean? What would I do now? I had never planned this as a solo trip. Those single-handed guys were nuts. And if they weren't when they set sail, they usually came back that way.

Then I was invited to a party onboard the *Carpe Diem*.

PART II

CHAPTER SEVENTEEN

January, 1962
Colon, Panama

"You new around here?"

The voice behind me came from a slim young girl. Her long blond hair hung smooth and silky down her back, the ends tossing in the breeze, grazing the waistband of her cutoff shorts. As I faced her I was drawn in to her big, glowing smile, and steady blue eyes. They stayed on mine, waiting my reply. The smell of coconut oil hung in the night air.

"Been here a couple of weeks. I'm on the *Gracias*, out of Annapolis." I gestured to her, a few berths away. "Oh, I'm Ken."

She took my hand and gave it a delicate shake, making a little mock curtsey with it.

"How do you do, Ken. I'm Patty."

"Nice to meet you. I've been looking at the rigging," I said, gesturing toward the mast. "Have you ever seen this boat sail?"

"No, I don't think so."

We were both guests at a party aboard the *Carpe Diem*, a seventy-five-foot yacht owned by Charlie Carson, an American who visited Panama every winter. I never met his crew, other than a steward, and after a time wondered if he actually sailed or just kept his yacht here, a floating second home.

"Me neither."

"You said you have a boat? Where are you headed?"

"Through the Canal, then on to the Galapagos; I'll probably make a stop in the Marquesas, then to the Society Islands. I hope to make them by May, and take a break there. I'm headed around the world." I added the last part proudly, in case she hadn't already put it together.

"That sounds fun!"

"I think so. We've been planning it for years."

"We? Are you traveling with your wife?"

I laughed. "No, I'm talking about my college buddy. But things didn't work out." It was the first time I'd said it out loud, and it smarted to remember BJ and Jean were gone.

"Funny, I thought about going to college, but I went sailing instead! Some friends invited me to go down to Baja. My dream is to see the world on a sailboat. To visit all those tropical ports and beaches." She smiled at me. "You know what I mean! Anyway, I don't know where I'm headed next. Anywhere, I suppose. I'm looking to join up with a boat sometime soon. I'm just itching to go somewhere, to get out of here."

She held up her near-empty martini glass. "To seeing the world!" I held up mine and they met with a glassy clink.

"If you need a first mate, I'm your girl. I can help with whatever you need, I've done it all."

"Really?" I assessed her petite frame.

"You bet! I can sail with both hands tied behind my back!" She laughed. "OK, maybe not. But almost. Just promise me you'll think about it?" Her eyes stayed on mine, her face lit with martinis and that big smile. "Charlie knows where to find me, if you're interested."

I was interested. Laying in my bunk that night I thought about it. She had gone on to tell me her father had a Rhodes 77; that was a fine boat. If she could handle that, she could surely help on the *Gracias*. She was friendly enough. And she really was a pretty thing. It might be fun to have her aboard.

I was ready to move on. My goal had been to leave Panama by New Year's Day, yet today was January 18th. Since BJ and Jean had left for California, I had dawdled here alone, losing time in the sunny days and the party-filled nights.

My challenge was to get through the Canal. Each yacht was required to have at least three crew on board, two to handle the ropes and one to be at the helm during the passage through the locks. Beyond that, I needed a crew to continue my journey around the world. It wasn't something I planned on doing solo.

Maybe Patty would be game for going at least to Panama City for a trial run. I'd be very clear upfront—she'd probably have to share the forward cabin with another crew member, and, most importantly, I couldn't pay anything, but would cover fuel and port expenses. She seemed like a pleasant gal. Disagreements at sea were the miserable end to many happy beginnings, but sometimes you have to take a chance. A three-night trial journey through the locks should be a good test. If it worked out, she could stay.

Throughout the region, there were guys for hire who would come on board for a few nights to assist in the

passage through the canal. While some might lack true
seamanship experience, they generally have their paperwork
in order, as the restrictions in the Canal Zone were always
tight; even more so now, with the heightened activity due
to the Cuba situation.

William Leahy was one of those guys; a slight and wiry
type, the kind you don't think much of at first, but I've
learned always turn out to be stronger than you imagine. He
had shaggy black hair and dark, serious eyes that made him
look part Indian. He was staying with my oddball neighbor
Woody in the marina between gigs. It seemed like a
dubious association, but then again, you never know what
you will find on the waterfront. When I learned he had
been through the canal eighteen times I worried less about
his choice of friends and instead thought about how I could
entice him to join me. He must have been having a slow
week; he agreed to do the passage for meals and all the beer
he could drink.

We set through the locks on January 28th. The *Gracias*
motored into Gatun, the first lock out of Shelter Bay.
Large, concrete waterways, like the culverts you see on land
to manage riverbeds and runoff, these wondrous feats of
technology astounded me every time. Ahead of us were two
other small crafts. Before the first was a seven-foot-thick
concrete gate. Longshoremen lined the banks, almost thirty
feet above the water line, ready to catch our ropes. Patty
tossed hers up with ease starboard, Leahy did the same
port; I kept the tiller steady. The longshoremen dallied their
lines around the cleats on the piers, keeping them slightly
taut. Once we had the "all clear," the concrete gates to the
lock slid closed behind the *Gracias*. We were in a swimming
pool of sorts; floating in water, enclosed by concrete on all
sides.

New water starting pouring into the chamber from culverts in the walls and the boats rose together. After about fifteen minutes we were almost level with the men on shore. The gate ahead of us eased open. The first yacht motored forward. Then the next. The longshoremen released the lines and threw them back aboard. Leahy and Patty coiled them up. I started the inboard and we gently pulled out of the lock, now at a higher elevation, into the lake ahead.

The locks connect a series of lakes, wide and sprawling in places. Beyond them were swampy estuaries and low jungle-covered hills. We had clear weather for the passage, which was fortunate. I'd been through many times during the rainy season, where the rain fell hard and thick like snow in a New England blizzard. It poured heavily on the water, splashing up to create a thick mist in the warm air. On deck you'd have to hold one hand above your nose and mouth to breathe. But for this voyage it was sunny and clear, and we could see for miles beyond the waterways across the vast jungle.

On the morning of the third day we motored out of Miraflores, the final lock, and into Playita Marina at Panama City. I was pleased with how everything went. I started thinking about the next phase of this journey. Would Patty and Leahy make a good crew for the long term?

I didn't know what class of seaman Leahy was or where he got his training. He never talked about his past. I decided to take him out for a sail to see what he could do.

The bay at Playita is crowded with sailboats, local fishing boats, ferries, and large cargo ships, some crossing the bay, some entering or exiting the Canal. Leahy deftly took us out around them, giving a wide, safe berth and keeping the *Gracias* steady through the many washes these ships left behind. After sailing across the bay as far as the point, he turned her easily and began a port tack back across, into the wind.

It was a good choice and he did a fine job managing his sails. Back near the marina we doused the fore and the main and sat for a bit before motoring in, smoking cigarettes while *Gracias* bobbed in the busy waters of the bay. The sky was turning gray; storm clouds were beginning to move from the low hills around Panama City and out over the water. We were in the midst of *verano*, the summer season down here, made rough by northerly winds and high swells.

"Looks like a storm's coming," said Leahy, judging the sky with somber eyes.

"I hear at least half a dozen times a year a boat's struck by lightning," I said.

"I've heard the same."

"So tell me, Leahy, where are you going from here?"

"What do you mean?" He turned to me with the same serious look.

"You plan to keep doing this canal work? Doesn't that get old? You know how to sail. Don't you want to catch some wind and quit all the motoring back and forth?"

"I don't know. All these guys coming through here have grand dreams of going around the world. No offense—I just don't know if I'm in for the long haul."

"Don't tell me you're afraid of the high seas?"

"Me? Naw, I love 'em. It's like riding a green horse. There are a couple of things you can predict will happen; for the rest of it you just hang on," he said, still straight-faced.

"Weak stomach?"

"Naw, none of that. I don't know, the longest I've been aboard in one stretch is three weeks and I'm OK with that for a record. You and Patty seem like you're set for a good voyage. I'm sure you two will have fun!" His dark eyes glimmered and he gave me a wink.

I laughed. "Well, maybe, but she just joined up for the Canal."

"A fine-looking thing like that would make any journey a lot more interesting."

"You bet."

He could rig and reef, and I saw how he kept an eye on the sails, watching the wind and water in tandem before making any adjustments. He'd shown me he knew the ropes and I kind of liked his easy attitude. I took a deep breath.

"You should come along. I can't pay you, but it'll get you out of the Canal Zone. At the very least on to somewhere else, get a change of view."

"Well, maybe." He looked at me, deadpan again. "Where you headed next? Galapagos?"

"Yes, then the Marquesas for a stop, on our way to the Society Islands, Samoa, Tahiti," I said and laughed. "You know, the usual route for us round-the-world dreamers."

He allowed a small nod to my joke but his face stayed indifferent. "When do you plan to set sail?"

"As soon as the wind is right and you say yes."

"Huh." It was a deep, one-syllable laugh, and I almost saw a small smile. "Well, I can't say I've gotten any better offers. OK, Captain." He held out a hand, looked me in the eye, and we shook on it. "When the wind is right."

Back in port we shared the news with Patty, and in a moment of glad-heartedness I asked her if she'd like to continue on as well. From what she had told me, she would be a capable sailor.

"Of course! I thought you'd never ask!" she said, and gave me a big hug and kiss on the cheek.

That evening the three of us celebrated with cold beers and grilled snapper on deck. After supper Leahy brought out his guitar and began a repertoire of country tunes. I joined him on my harmonica. Patty sung along when she knew the words, clapping a hand against her beer bottle.

Most sailors are an easygoing bunch, having learned to get along within close quarters, and used to meeting new people at every port. These two were no different, and looked like they would easily adapt to life aboard the *Gracias*. I had them share the spacious forward cabin, well fitted with three bunks and ample storage. I tried to make them feel at home. And I tried to regenerate my initial excitement for this adventure. I missed BJ and Jean and our jokes and teasing. But a new chapter lay before me. I was committed to continuing on, to try the *Gracias* on the great Pacific, to see her make her way around the globe. If it meant taking on a new crew, so be it. She and I were in accord; we would adapt and make our way as needed. This was my hope.

That hope would change my course, my destiny, indeed, my entire life and the lives of those I had yet to encounter.

CHAPTER EIGHTEEN

February, 1962
Playita, Panama

"You sure, Captain?"

"Yes, I'm sure."

"You're sure you're sure?"

"Yes."

"Because you know we'll have ours… but we're only getting enough for us."

"I know."

Leahy chimed in to Patty's questioning. "And you can't get any in the Galapagos. From what I've heard they just have a little trading post with fruit and stuff."

"Yeah, I've heard the same. I'll be fine. Get what you're getting and let's get out of here."

Their concern was annoying. I'd made up my mind; they didn't have to try to change it.

"It's at least three weeks to there, plus another three to the Marquesas," Leahy added.

"Yes, I'm well aware."

The Chinese shop owner waiting on us was dressed in a shirt and tie under a blue work coat. The coat had wide arms and was wrapped snuggly with a cloth belt at the waist. He stood watching our debate, patiently waiting for a decision. Eight red-and-white cases of Marlboros lay on the counter. Leahy nodded at them.

"*Ocho cajas? Algo mas?*" the shop owner asked in perfect Spanish.

"No, just these," Leahy replied. He looked at me one more time. "You're sure?"

"Yes, I'm sure!" I said, and I started toward the door.

A moment later Leahy and Patty joined me on the sidewalk. Leahy carried their purchase in a paper bag. Patty was holding a banana.

"It's not too late if you change your mind, Captain." Patty looked up at me with her broad smile. "We're not leaving till tomorrow."

I laughed. "You two just don't believe me, do you?" We walked back toward the marina.

"I don't understand why you'd want to quit. There's nothing wrong with smoking. It's fun."

"All men do it, from cowboys to sailors to country singers," said Leahy.

"Well, they're saying it causes lung damage."

"Since when?" said Patty, peeling her banana.

"We learned about it in school. Anyway, they always said that an officer smokes a pipe, cigarettes are for the common seaman." I gave her a wink. "I might take up the pipe when we get to the Marquesas. It's full of Frenchmen, I bet they smoke pipes. Don't worry; I won't bum any off you."

"You better not!" She took a bite of the banana.

"I promise. What's with the banana?"

"What do you mean?"

"You're not bringing that on board, are you?" I looked at Leahy.

"I told you, Patty, Captain won't allow it. They're bad luck."

"Bananas? You guys are crazy!" she made loopy circles with the banana around her ear. "Why would a banana be bad luck?" Another bite. The cursed thing was almost gone.

"They just are. It's been known among sailors and fishermen for centuries. I'm not going to push our luck now. Not on this voyage," I said.

"That's the craziest thing I've ever heard!"

Now we were in the marina, nearing the long pier where the *Gracias* was docked among dozens of other vessels. It wouldn't do for other crews to see her sashaying through with that banana in her hand.

"Are you done?" I gestured toward the almost empty peel.

She took a last bite and, holding the peel upside down by the tip, flagrantly swung it toward a nearby trash bin. It somersaulted through the air, yellow flaps flailing like the wings of a distressed bird, and finally, with relief, landed in the bin.

It was already a risk, traveling with a woman. Neptune didn't like that. She didn't need to push her luck with that stupid banana.

Early the next morning we motored out of Playita under fair skies, bound for the Galapagos. I stood at the helm while Leahy worked the winch. We observed the variety of yachts and ships docked in the flat harbor. It felt like leaving Annapolis again; I was excited to sail on the open sea once more. Even Leahy had a lighthearted look, his dark hair tossed by the breeze, his eyes keen on the breakwater. Patty popped up on deck.

"Good morning!" She went over to Leahy and gave him a big smile. "Got a light?" His hands were full with the winch but he locked it for a moment, dug in his pocket, and pulled out a pack of matches. Patty leaned into Leahy with a cigarette between her puckered lips. He lit it, and she inhaled, giving him a big smile. She turned to greet me.

"Hey, Captain Ken. It's take-off time!"

"That was at 0600, but yes, we're departing now."

"How far are we going, again?"

"You mean to reach the Galapagos?"

"Yeah, there." She blew a length of smoke out the corner of her mouth.

"It's over 800 nautical miles."

"What are 'nautical miles'?" she asked, as easily as if she were wondering, "What should we make for lunch?"

I looked at her sideways. "Nautical miles? You know, how we measure things at sea. One nautical mile is 1,852 meters, in case you forgot."

"I never knew that. Why do they use those?"

Leahy glanced over at me.

This was standard sailing terminology, and everyone who used it knew why. Maybe Patty's father hadn't bothered to explain it to her.

"Well, it has to do with the curvature of the Earth. Since it's not flat, they don't use regular miles. Rather, this represents one minute of arc along a meridian." She wrinkled her eyebrows together and her eyes squinted as if in concentration. "You know, those lines that go up and down on the globe?" I asked. She said nothing. I explained further. "It's a standard measure, regardless of how the Earth might be more or less wide at any point."

She took another deep drag on the cigarette and her eyes widened. When she exhaled, she exclaimed, "Oh, of course, meridians!" like it had just slipped her mind. Patty gave a big smile like all was dandy. "Thanks for reminding me again, Captain Ken!"

She tossed the rest of the cigarette over the rail. "I need a cup of coffee." She headed below.

It didn't matter to her that she couldn't understand the nautical mile. I couldn't believe it. These were facts that she should know; they had direct bearing on our lives. It was the science and math that made our journey possible. How could she not care? Her attitude was as incomprehensible to me as the superstition about bananas was to her.

Patty said she was interested in learning celestial navigation, or as she called it, "astrology," and I agreed to teach her, thinking maybe this was an area she could be of use. The more hands we had with these skills the better. We sat at the aft deck late one night while I was on watch. I had her sit next to me, close, so we could both look from the same vantage point to the constellations I pointed out above.

"OK, so starting with Corvus. Do you see that off-shaped rectangle? Right there?" She leaned in and looked down the length of my arm. "It's called Corvus, or 'crow.' There are four points, the left top star is a little higher than the right."

"Wait, let me see… yes, I see it!" She turned away and took a long drag on her cigarette, then stretched her arm out to hold it far from her body. She blew out a long stream of smoke in the same direction. Her pack of Marlboros lay on the deck next to her.

It was intoxicating. That sweet burn of tobacco, and the warm, rich smoke. I wanted one.

We were six days out of Panama. I smelled Leahy and Patty's cigarettes whenever they smoked on deck. At first, they had given me a lot of distance when they smoked, moving aft to the lee of the boat. "It's OK," I assured them, "I'm fine." And it was OK. It was. For a few days. Then I started to dream about smoking. Holding a cigarette in between my fingers, letting the smoke drift around my head, and taking a deep, long drag. I'd wake from these dreams at first excited, then anxious and sad about the reality of my situation.

Tonight, the craving was too much for me to bear. My lungs yearned for the warm burning sensation. My fingers twitched with anticipation.

Patty cocked her head toward my shoulder. "Crow, OK, what else is there?"

I put my left hand behind her on the deck, and leaned back, looking up. Her hair tickled my arm.

"OK, make a line directly to the right of the top right corner. That bright star there? That's the tip of Virgo. Spica."

"Um, OK... yes!"

I crept my hand around her behind, toward her left hip. I had to take her gaze further away.

"OK, and from there, see how there's a star that way? Together they make a line." I pointed my finger, gesturing back and forth between the stars to indicate a line.

"OK."

My fingertips had grazed the edge of the pack. I took a gentle, quiet hold of it, and gave it a shake. Patty wouldn't mind if I borrowed a smoke.

"And from there, we can see two stars below the first one, and if you imagine lines connecting them, it looks like the legs of an animal."

"I guess I see it." She took another drag.

"Virgo is the second largest constellation. Hydra is the biggest. Spica means 'ear of grain'; the constellation used to be referred to as a 'furrow,' like when they are growing wheat in a field." I glanced at Patty's face; it had a glazed-over look. Two cigarettes had slipped out of the square opening in the top of the pack and lay beneath my hand. I gently put it down. Patty's left arm swung out over my hand, and she blindly leaned to her left to toss her spent cigarette under the rail. That was close.

"You see there?" I pointed even further east, making her lean into me, and away from her left side. "That's the entire constellation of Virgo."

"Virgo?" She thought for a minute, then looked up into my face and smiled. "I know all about Virgos."

Now I had two precious cigarettes in the palm of my hand. "Oh yeah, what do you know?"

"Well, my ex-boyfriend was a Virgo. He could sure talk! And he was always nitpicky about every little thing. Everything had to be perfect for him."

I eased my hand behind her back, cigarettes delicately cupped there, careful not to crush them. Where the heck was I going to put them?

"Really?"

"Oh yeah, he was bossy too. But he was a really good surfer."

I leaned on the heel of my hand, sweat building in my palm. A steamy, tobacco-filled cave.

"Hey, where'd my smokes go?" Patty patted her right hand down between us, then her left, where she found her cigarettes there. She picked it up and shook one out. "I don't know how you don't want one of these, Captain Ken."

She shook the pack, and peered at it. "Dang!"

I held my breath.

"I had my matches right here, didn't I?" She usually tucked a book of matches into the plastic wrap around the pack. It was missing.

She glanced around the deck. "I'll be right back."

She hopped up and went to the companionway. "Billy!" she called, looking for him below.

I popped the two smokes in my right breast pocket. Just in time. My hand had been going numb pressed there against the deck. I shook it out for a moment. Once the two of them were asleep I could smoke one. Maybe just half. I'd be conservative with my stash.

CHAPTER NINETEEN

February 19, 1962
Location: 1° 10' 35" N
                  88° 25' 6" W

A scream from the galley woke me.

I popped out of my bunk and went to the salon. Patty stood in the middle of the small space with her mouth gaping, standing still as a statue. Beans in a half-cooked state covered the galley ceiling and trickled down the nearest wall. They slid across the floor in wide, muddy-looking swaths, back and forth with the roll of the boat. A brown slime dripped from the ceiling on to the floor between me and Patty.

Her eyes were wide. "I don't know what happened. Everything was fine when I turned on the stove." She shrugged, hands to the ceiling, confused.

I had come down into the salon earlier that afternoon after Leahy took over watch. Patty was at the galley counter pouring water into the pressure cooker pot.

"Hey, Captain."

"Hello. What you got there?"

"I thought I'd put on some pinto beans. I don't think I could stand to eat another can of soup tonight."

Beans did sound good. We had a cache of salted pork and some potatoes that would make it a good meal. "Have you used one of those before?"

"Sure, piece of cake. Just get the water boiling and set it here, they should be done in an hour. Don't worry, Captain!"

"All right. Watch the regulator. If you have the heat too high you're going to have problems."

"Of course!" she said, giving me her winning smile.

Of course, everyone knew that. I was drowsy from my four-hour watch in the hot sun. I headed aft to my cabin for a nap.

And now we faced this mess.

A spout of beans had taken off from inside the pressure cooker, through the vent pipe, and straight up to the ceiling. It was clear Patty hadn't put the regulator correctly in place on the lid vent. Subsequently when the pressure increased in the pot, the beans tried to escape the only place they could—through the small hole in the lid. I looked at her.

"I thought you knew how to use a pressure cooker?"

"How hard could it be? You turn it on and it cooks everything in there, right?"

I rubbed my hand over my face, looking down at the floor. I shook my head.

"Clean it up."

"Sure, get me a bucket, would you?"

"No, I won't. Clean it up yourself, Patty."

"There's no need to be angry with me. I was just trying to help. Everyone's sick of eating those damn cans of soup, you know. Half of them don't even have a label; you can't tell what's in them. I was trying to make a decent dinner for once."

"Sure, but if that were the case, you should have asked me how to use the damn pressure cooker, for God's sake." My voice was rising, and I let it. I was sick of eating soup too. Now having beans for dinner was no longer an option. They were all over the floor. It was completely unnecessary; she could have asked me for help. I should have done it myself. Leahy popped his head down the passageway.

"What's going on?"

"Cap't Ken's mad at me. I was just trying to make us a nice dinner."

Adding fuel to my fire wasn't a good idea. Didn't she know I was in charge here?

I took a deep breath. I couldn't bow to her silly games or be baited. I was the captain. I needed to act like it.

"Patty had an accident with the pressure cooker. She's cleaning it up now."

"And he won't help me. Billy, can you get me a bucket?"

"Patty, Billy is on watch. He needs to get back to the helm. You're to clean this up yourself. All of it. I don't want to find a bean anywhere."

Leahy glanced at me and promptly went back on deck.

Patty looked at me with a pouty expression and those flat, calm eyes.

I went back to my cabin and let her deal with her mess. I lay on my bunk, staring at the ceiling. This situation, along with the inside of the *Gracias*, was a disaster. We'd only been at sea two and a half weeks and I was having doubts about how we could succeed any further. Patty was a lazy, spoiled brat who only had designs on getting her own way. And she wasn't very bright either. She needed to shape up and start to perform as a reliable crew member, or we were going to have problems.

Early the next morning as the sun cleared the horizon I took a reading with my sextant. I knew we were close to the Galapagos. I consulted my charts and, indeed, we should arrive there by the next day. The equator was within spitting distance.

Crossing the magical equator is a rite of passage for all sailors. It is an invisible, intangible line that exists only in the minds of men yet governs every physical law of navigation. Crossing it means you are no longer a "pollywog" but are promoted into the world of "shellbacks." Celebrations for this milestone varied across cultures and vessels. Many ships held tributes to Neptune, god of the sea. A "court" of shellbacks was created and the "wogs," as we called them, had to come before it, standing trial for their crimes against the sea. These might include disregard for the power of the almighty Neptune or harming creatures from the sea. Neptune would only be appeased by a guilty plea and show of submission. It was common tradition for the veteran shellbacks to tease and torment the "wogs" and make them go through hazing ceremonies to show their obedience to Neptune. On big ships initiation rituals could be elaborate affairs of pranks, tests, and trials that started the afternoon before the crossing and went on through the night. While they may have seemed silly and strange to anyone on land, these ceremonies were a bonding time for crews and broke the monotony of long days and sea.

In contrast, a solo sailor might simply light a cigar in celebration and tip a shot of whiskey into the sea as a tribute to gain Neptune's favor. What was vital with all ceremonies was that they were timed to coincide with sunset.

On a forty-foot vessel it's difficult to hide, but in truth I hadn't seen Patty since the previous day. I knew she was lying low after the bean fiasco. Leahy had been keeping a testy eye on me too. I decided that considering the state of mind of our crew, a crossing ceremony was the perfect activity to bring some levity to the current situation and boost morale all around.

I had long been a shellback, since my first trip to South America. Leahy and Patty had never been this far south. They were still wogs.

"I'm a what?"

"A pollywog, Patty. Until we cross the equator tonight."

"OK, cool! Is that when we start the party?"

"After the crossing ceremony. You and Billy are going to be initiated."

"Into what?"

"One of the most elite clubs of sailors. You will be a shellback!"

"What? Why would I want to be one of those?"

"Patty, it's a thing sailors do. You know, to show they've been around. That they've crossed the equator. It's considered a badge of honor," Leahy said.

"Oh. Shellback?"

"Yes, that's what it's called. You will have to succumb to the will of Neptune and appease any mistakes you've made against him." I looked at the sky. We were an hour from dark. "Let's get started. Line up here."

I had the two of them stand at the stern, backs to the water, facing me.

"Now first, you have to admit to any trespasses you may have made against Neptune. Have you done any of the following: sailed across the sea without regard for the wishes of Neptune; eaten creatures from the sea; or polluted the sea?"

Patty had a worried look.

"Yes, sir," Leahy said. He knew how this worked.

"Well, no, not really," Patty said. "I don't believe I've gone against Neptune's wishes. I mean, what are they anyway? And I know I haven't eaten any creatures. Yuck!"

I laughed. "What about the fish we've eaten?"

"Well, those are fish, not creatures."

"It's the same thing," Leahy said under his breath.

"Oh, I guess. Then my answer's yes."

"Now, having admitted to your crimes against Neptune, you must succumb to his demands." This was the fun part. "On your hands and knees."

Leahy dropped to the ground. Patty looked at me.

"What?"

"Go ahead, get down."

"Why? What are we doing?"

"Just follow my orders."

On her knees, she looked sideways at Leahy. He kept his eyes on me, waiting for my next command.

"Now, circumnavigate the *Gracias*, on hands and knees."

"What are we supposed to do?"

"Follow me." Leahy took off toward the starboard side.

"Really? OK!" Suddenly excited, Patty laughed and went quickly after Leahy.

It was a silly exercise, but innocent fun compared to what I had seen on other ships. Some men used these rituals to get even with crewmembers they had a beef with; others to take out the aggressions they had accumulated during their days away at sea. In the name of fun and games, far from any official authority and the naïve scrutiny of those on land, they had their way with the wogs. They subjected them to all sorts of torture; abuses of the sort that can only be conjured by those who have spent months of tediously similar days at sea and have had lots of time to think.

While Patty and Leahy made their way toward the bow I dipped two five-gallon buckets into the sea, filling each of them and setting them on deck.

Leahy arrived back first, and stayed down on his hands and knees. Patty came alongside him.

"Good job, mates, I think Neptune is starting to forgive you. But we have to do one more thing. Stand up." They stood before me. "Turn around." They faced aft.

"Be prepared to be washed of all your sins and trespasses!" I proclaimed.

I picked up a bucket and gleefully lifted it over Patty's head. She squealed and jumped when the water hit. "Aagh!!!" I can't say I felt bad about soaking her.

Leahy, of course, knew what was coming and took his quick bath with ease.

"Nice job. You have now earned your membership in the Shellback society. Now, we celebrate!"

We moved to the forward deck, where we could watch the sun sink into the sea ahead of us. I poured us each a shot of whiskey and handed out the glasses.

"To Neptune! May he bless us with fair seas, a good wind, and a companionable voyage." We each threw back a shot. I poured another round.

"To Neptune!" Patty added, "Thanks for the fish!"

CHAPTER TWENTY

March 1, 1962
Location: 2° 16' 24" S
            90° 45' 18" W

We were back at sea after a week's rest in the Galapagos. There we had enjoyed our time on land and among creatures that didn't swim, chasing quick little iguanas across the fields of black lava rocks and, in contrast, observing the still, large, lumbering tortoises. They were everywhere—hidden among the rocks that edged the beaches, solemnly tucked under a rough piece of bush. At first it felt like a trick of the eye; what you thought was a big, steady boulder suddenly moved. Most stunning about these islands were the sea lions, who lay stretched out alongside the tidal pools sunning their golden, silky coats and chatting among themselves with their strange barking voices.

Stealing was something I'd never imagined myself doing. But I was desperate. We'd all been right—there was limited commerce and no cigarettes for sale in port. I thought I would be over it by now, but the craving for tobacco had taken over my mind. When I set the rigging, I thought, "It would be great to have a smoke after this." Then I remembered. It was always energizing to have a cigarette in hand to start the midnight watch. But I had none. Long days, and all through the even longer nights. We were still three weeks from the Marquesas.

I didn't know where Patty kept hers, but Leahy had his extra packs on a high shelf tucked behind the door of their cabin, along with a few pints of that rot-gut liquor he bought in the Galapagos. Sweat building on my forehead, I slipped into the cabin alone. Leahy was at the helm on the noon to 1600 shift, Patty likely sunbathing nearby. I quickly moved around the door to face the shelf. The case on top was open, a few packs remaining. I took the one below it, still full. Holding it in my hand, I pulled a razor blade from my pocket. With a quick, straight pull I made a cut in the cellophane wrapper at the end of the case. I pulled it back gently, making it tear a bit, until I got my fingers into the edge of the box. I pulled open the end. Ah. The stacks of cigarette packs. Abundant with pure tobacco bliss. I slipped one out.

My left hand was sweaty around the box as I closed up the end of it. The plastic wrap couldn't be fixed, but it looked like an innocent tear made from the wear and travel in cargo ships over long seas, being tossed to and fro by delivery boys, and finally carried in a paper bag to this small boat. Sweat was building on my temples. I gave the box a stiff shake sideways to rebalance the packs inside and stacked it back on the shelf, under the open case.

I heard footsteps on the deck above me. Patty was moving about. I had to get out of here. Stepping out of their cabin, I took five long steps across the salon to reach mine at the rear. I closed the door behind me and leaned against it. I took a deep sniff of the pack, rich with its warm tobacco smell. Ah, that was nice.

There was a knock on the door, a bright "Shave-and-a-haircut" tap just behind my back. Patty's voice came through the thin wood as clearly as if she were standing beside me. "Hey, Captain."

"Yeah?" I called back, and looked about the cabin for a quick hiding place. My rubber boots stood there alongside my footlocker. I stepped over and slid the pack inside one of them. I pulled a pair of socks from a drawer and stuffed them in on top of it. No one would look there. I exhaled in relief that it was done, even if it would be an antsy six hours before I could have a smoke.

I quickly stepped back to the door and opened it.

"Hey." She looked at me, then down at the floor. "I was wondering, well, Billy and I were talking, and he thought, I mean, we thought maybe I should ask your advice. You know, in cooking and things. I know those beans didn't turn out like we wanted." She looked up and smiled. Cooking lessons? That was the last thing on my mind. But I was used to Patty's non sequiturs.

"OK, sure. You mean you want to learn how to use the pressure cooker?"

"Yeah, that would be a start. You know, on my dad's boat we didn't cook much. I don't think he really knew how! All we ever ate were bologna sandwiches. There wasn't much of a galley either."

I raised my eyebrows.

"Yeah, I know, it wasn't a Rhodes 77. That was just what he always dreamed of having. He had some old twenty-two-footer he pulled out of the scrap yard. And he did, he fixed it up good. Repaired the leaky portside hull, and painted it a bright orange, he said so people could see us from shore if we ever had an emergency. The other side was white. He ran out of paint," she explained, "so we'd just have to turn the boat around if something happened. But the sails, they were bright too! Any old canvas he found, he made into a sail. He'd raise them just for decoration sometimes, on holidays and such. Every Christmas I asked for a tree, but there was no room. It was just us and all our stuff, filling up the boat. You know, a twenty-two-footer doesn't have a lot of space. After my mom left we lived onboard full time." Her eyes gazed away, flat beneath, lost in her memories. "'Why pay rent when living on the boat is practically free?' he said. It was an adventure, that's what he said. It was just crowded. And one day we'd take her sailing. One day, once he found a tiller. We never had one, you know? He searched all the junkyards, looking for one that he could use. I'd come home from school and ask, 'Did you find it?' and he always said, 'Not today, honey, not today. But I'll be looking again tomorrow.' And he'd look, he sure did." Her eyes came back to the moment and looked at me. "But he never found one. And the Rhodes, well, that was docked down the pier a ways, by the other nice boats in the yacht club. We walked by it all the time, tied up there at the end of the pier, 'like royalty,' my dad would say, 'she's the Queen of the Pier.'" She smiled at me. "So, no, we didn't have a pressure cooker."

I stood with my hand still on the inside knob of the door while she shared this revelation. Her story explained a lot. But I wasn't entirely forgiving her just yet. We could start with cooking lessons.

"OK, meet me in the galley at 1400 and we'll get something started for supper tonight."

That broad smile filled her round face. "Yes, Captain!"

Maybe this would be a chance to make a decent crew member out of Patty. Then I laughed at the thought. She still couldn't identify a star to guide us, didn't care to understand the nautical mile, and always tied the wrong knots. But if she could learn to cook, it might be her saving grace.

That night we cooked up an exquisite supper on the grill, with baked potatoes and two varieties of grilled fish. Patty took delight in arranging everything nicely on the plates like in a fancy restaurant. We ate together up on deck while Leahy stood his watch. After dinner Patty took the dirty dishes downstairs.

"Not bad, Captain," said Leahy.

"Yeah, nothing like a home-cooked meal."

"How about some dessert?" Patty came through the companionway waving a bottle of Abuelo in her hand. I recognized it as the bottle of rum I bought weeks ago at Ezequiel's in Colon. Now it was battered and worn, like it had endured a rough passage.

"Where did you find that?"

"In the locker above the extra bunk in our cabin. I heard something clunking around and look! We got lucky!"

She set three glasses before us and poured a round.

That was odd to me, that it would have been in their cabin. Maybe I'd put it there and forgotten. I was sure it wasn't left there by my former crew; Jean was no drinker and BJ surely wasn't up to it in his last days.

"*Salud!*" Leahy said, raising his glass with his left hand, right still on the tiller.

"*Salud!*" I replied, and tipped back my shot. Patty had already drunk hers and was pouring another.

"*Salud?* Is that 'cheers' when you're at sea?"

"It means 'to your health.' It's Spanish," Leahy explained.

"*Salud!*" She held up her second shot and poured it easily down.

Patty lit a cigarette and took a long drag. She teased us through the smoke of her exhale, "I'm one ahead of you guys! You better hurry and catch up!"

Leahy laughed, "Oh, I'll catch up; I'm not worried about that." He gestured toward her to pour him another shot.

I could go for another myself, but I knew I'd be taking over for Leahy shortly. And he knew his shift was nearing its end. He tossed his head back dramatically, throwing the rum down his throat.

"Ahg! That hit the spot." He faced forward and shook his head hard, black shaggy hair flying about, like a wet dog that had just come in from the rain.

Patty poured another round for three. She swayed slightly from her seat on a locker as she reached out to hand me a glass. "Here ya go, Captain!"

One more wouldn't hurt.

"All together now," Patty said. She held her glass high above her seat on the deck. Leahy raised his left hand, right still on the tiller, and I joined with my glass. "*Salud!*"

A big smile on her face, she sat staring into space, her eyes squinting with satisfaction. Her cigarette was burning down, a long ash hanging unattended. I nodded toward it.

"Don't let that fall on the deck."

"Oops! Sorry, Captain!" She stood up abruptly, and with a surge sideways, stepped toward the rail. She leaned over in an exaggerated fashion, sure to ash the cigarette clear of the deck. It fell off into the water. She stayed there, clinging onto the rail, swaying forward over the edge of the deck and back again.

"It sure is pretty out here," she mused.

"Yes, it is. But why don't you come back this way and have a seat?" I was nervous watching her standing there, already drunk, with only the slim line of the rail between her and the water. A sudden swell could send her overboard.

"Yes, Captain!" She picked her way across the deck, arms swinging side to side for balance, and went back to her seat.

Leahy was sitting down, his arm loosely dropped over the tiller, cigarette hanging from one hand, empty shot glass in the other. It was time for me to take over for the night.

They stayed on deck with me, smoking cigarettes like it was going out of style and passing the bottle between them. There was no need for glasses any longer.

Hydra had long cleared the horizon when they decided to head below. They made their way down the companionway, Patty carrying the empty bottle tucked under her arm. I heard a loud thump, followed by her laughter, and Leahy's loud "shushing" sounds. Then more laughter. At least they didn't have a long way to stumble home.

It was convenient that they shared a cabin and took to spending their free time together. Over the weeks they had become as thick as thieves. I never saw one without the other. I was pleased to have Patty out of my hair; Leahy didn't seem to mind her hanging around him at the helm. In the beginning I hoped maybe she was learning some things. They took all their watches together, but in reality, I knew Leahy was doing all the work. And Patty liked it that way. They retired together at midnight, leaving the toughest shift for me: 0000 to 0400.

Once they were settled in for the night I had my solace in a stolen cigarette and the constellations.

I thought about our situation. Far from my original plans of a capable team of three, this crew had devolved to a lazy teenage girl and a simple drunk cowboy who had gone soft on her. Taking them on had been a risk to begin with, and now it felt like a catastrophic mistake. She'd almost tumbled in the drink tonight. Attempting a man-overboard rescue, all three of us a little drunk on rum, could have been a deadly disaster.

There was an idea bouncing around in my mind that I had to address. I looked out over the dark sea and took a deep pull on my cigarette.

At Kings Point they taught us that sailing alone went against maritime law. The law requires every vessel have a proper look-out at all times to prevent collision, ensuring the safety of your vessel and others at sea. It's impossible for a solo sailor on a long haul to do this. The need to sleep, chart your course, and tend to other duties takes you away from the helm. Enthusiasts of solo sailing argue that when crossing a large body of water, like the Pacific, there is little chance of collision. But it has happened. After working aboard large cargo ships, I know for a fact we can't see everything that is happening on the water below. I would hate for the *Gracias* to be splintered by a 2,000-ton cargo ship, and me with her.

Besides the legalities, I couldn't ignore the dozens of fanciful tales I read about the sea. Strange sightings of unknown creatures, gloomy ghost ships with their ghost captains, and the ships that disappear altogether. I had heard many stories of solo sailors seeing apparitions; the way they told it, these strangers appeared real, not ghosts at all, but solid in form and flesh. Often the skippers had long, deep conversations with their visitors, and in at least one story, shared a meal. Of course, the accounts were told only by the afflicted; no witness could verify nor deny that they happened. I didn't put much stock in the fantasies and stories from old timers. I was young, fit, strong of mind and will; I knew going to sea as an exercise in discipline and focus. Yet the tales of the supernatural were haunting, lingering in my mind like the ghost stories I heard as a boy around the campfire.

I tossed the cigarette butt into the sea and looked out over the dark water toward the Marquesas Islands, still many days away. While it wasn't my preference to sail alone, it was looking like the better of my options.

I could only blame myself for my predicament, captain over all this foolishness. And only I could fix it.

CHAPTER TWENTY-ONE

Date: March 27, 1962
Location: Bay of Traitors, Marquesas Islands

I was scrambling eggs in bacon grease when Leahy came into the salon. His dark hair stood up all over his head; a day's beard showed on his face. This was normal living on a boat. But his eyes were squinty and bloodshot.

"Rough night?" I teased.

"Oh yeah."

"Some breakfast might help."

"Coffee?" he asked.

I poured him a mug from the pot on the stove.

He took it and sat on the bench with a heavy oomph. He didn't look in the mood for conversation.

"You're up early, for someone with a rough night behind him." He and Patty had stumbled back aboard near 0200 this morning.

"I smelled the bacon. Had to get up. Just like back home. Bacon's frying, it's time to get up. At the house or in camp on a cattle drive. Don't need no alarm clock. Just bacon."

I had to laugh at this reliance on his nose. But soon I took a deep breath and went back to my feelings of consternation. I had stayed up late the night before, contemplating, and had come to my verdict. I had valid points and examples to support each of them. I looked at Leahy, taking a long, innocent slurp of his coffee. It wasn't my fault. He had put himself in this situation.

It was time to break it to him. His red eyes and draggy attitude lent itself well to my argument. I scooped the cooked eggs out of the pan and onto a plate.

"Want some?"

He made a face. "No, thanks. Just 'cause I can smell breakfast doesn't mean I want it every morning. Especially today."

"OK. Where's Patty? Sleeping it off?"

"Yeah."

"Great. We can talk." I faced him with the empty frying pan in my hand. I took a breath. "I'll be taking the next leg solo."

"What do you mean? Taking a trip over to Nuku Hiva?"

"No, I'll be leaving the Marquesas. Today."

"What?"

"Yes. Things aren't working out with our crew." I turned to put the pan in the sink, then faced him across the counter. "I think it's best you and Patty find another boat for your next passage."

"Aw, come on, Captain. I know we've been having fun since we got to Hiva Oa. But that's just 'cause we're in port. We'll straighten out once we're at sea."

"No, you won't. And it's not just at port. This has been going on since we left Panama City." He looked dumbfounded for a moment. He raised an eyebrow.

"This is about her, isn't it? What, are you jealous?"

I laughed. "You can keep that spoiled brat. But she is part of the problem. She hasn't been doing shit around here and you've been trying to cover her ass. And on our passage from the Galapagos—going overboard—what the hell was that? She put herself, and all of us, in harm's way. She's a danger to the voyage, and you know it. This expedition was designed for a crew of three. Three capable people. You'd be OK, Billy, believe me. But with her around, it's not working."

"What do you mean? I've stood all my watches. Done all my chores. A bunch of hers too. Doesn't that count for something?"

"Yes, I've noticed. Don't let a woman become your downfall, man. Didn't your father ever tell you that?"

"My downfall? Her? That's bullshit. I've been doing this for years. You have a 'capable crew.' You just don't like us because we're not from 'The Academy,' like you and your other crew. Not everyone gets the chance to go to school, you know. Hell, some of us don't even need it. You're just another stuck-up, East Coast asshole."

He put down his mug and went to the forward cabin. Before I could sit down to eat, Patty came careening out of the cabin, a white T-shirt of Leahy's billowing around her small frame. She leaned across the counter toward me, her hands on either side of my breakfast plate.

"You can't kick us off! We have an agreement. We've been busting our asses on this boat. Your boat! And all for you, we've been helping you this whole time, for free, we haven't gotten a penny out of it."

She wasn't going down without a fight. "Your passage from Colon to here doesn't count for something?" I tried not to laugh. "And please describe for me how you've been 'busting your ass?' Is that what you call it when you're smoking cigarettes on the forward deck all day long?"

"We need to have a break too, you know. You work us to death on this miserable boat." She looked back at Leahy, standing in the cabin door. "Especially him, he's been doing back-to-back watches since we left the Galapagos."

"Yes, he has. And he knows why, if you don't. It sounds like you should be glad to be leaving."

"You can't do this, just leave us in the middle of nowhere! I'm reporting you! We'll file a complaint at the harbor master's. We'll have your license taken away. You better like living on this boat, you'll never work at sea again!"

I looked at Leahy. He was facing the floor, trying to hide his laugh at her ridiculous threat.

"Well, that's a mean thing to do to someone who helped saved your life." Had she already forgotten that day?

"You just did it so you could hold it over my head. Just for a time like this. You didn't really mean it."

She was a real piece of work. My face got hot. In a stiff voice I said, "Get your stuff and go."

"Just like that, you're kicking us off?"

"Yes, I am. I'm captain of this vessel, and it's my prerogative." My voice was loud now. I looked directly into her flat blue eyes on the other side of the counter, still containing Leahy's coffee mug and my plate of bacon and eggs. I was tempted to reach across it and slap her tan face.

"What an asshole. Wait until I tell my dad about this!"

The tension of the morning had been building since I cracked the first eggs. Knowing I was going to have to give them their leave today had worn on me. Her insolent comments added fuel to the fire. But that, there, threatening to tell her father, like the whiny, childish bitch that she was, that broke through the tension. I fell back against the counter and bent over, my body shaking with laughter. We were on a tiny island five thousand miles away from her hometown. She was going to tell her father on me? The guy who lived on a boat with no rudder? I leaned back for a big gulp of air, and came forward and laughed some more. My body was shaking, tears were filling my eyes. I was gasping for breath. It was terrific.

Patty made a dramatic spin that flung her long hair hard and fast around the room. She stepped around Leahy and back into their cabin. I was sure it wasn't the first time she'd stormed out of a room amid peals of a man's laughter. And, God help her, it probably wouldn't be the last.

William Leahy was a man of the plains and the sea; accustomed to changes that came with the wind, he was already at the cabin door with his duffel packed. He moved smartly to the head to take his toothbrush and razor. Squatting to tuck them away in his bag he looked up at me with bloodshot eyes.

"You sure about this, Captain?" He straightened up. "I know she's a pain in the ass. But how are you going to continue single-handed? The *Gracias* isn't exactly designed for that." He made a covert look toward the cabin door and dropped his voice. "I can see leaving her behind, but what about me? The two of us? We can do it. You know I can crew this vessel."

The laughter had diffused much of my tension and, wiping tears from the corners of my eyes, I looked at him calmly.

"Billy, you're right on many counts, and I'm sorry to leave you in this position. But you should have thought of that before you got involved with that little piece of trouble. You had lots of opportunities to straighten her out. How do I know it won't happen again, with someone else? In my mind, you're as big of a liability as she is."

His face became dark with anger, and maybe shame. He looked at the floor. "Fine. Fair winds to you, Captain." He called back toward the cabin. "Patty?! Let's go!"

She stomped over the threshold, straight through the salon to the companionway. There she struggled to keep her big overstuffed bag over her shoulder as she climbed the narrow steps. Leahy tried to take it from her, but she ignored him and held it tight, looking over his head to give me one last hateful glare. She clambered out the hatch and onto the deck. Leahy followed, lanky and with ease. I followed the both of them; I wanted to make sure they departed without any further trouble.

Patty hopped off the *Gracias* and strode quickly down the pier, leaning slightly forward under the weight of her bag. Leahy followed a few paces behind. Whatever they did next was no longer any concern of mine.

The sun had risen; it looked like it would be a pleasant day in this "Bay of Traitors." Low green mountains circled this pretty bay, home to a picturesque little port town. But I wouldn't have time for sightseeing. Not on this trip at least.

It was time for me to go. There was no need to sit here at dock and wait to hear the gossip come back to me. I was sure Patty would tell everyone what a mean, vile captain I was. She would have to, if she expected anyone to take her on board again. As for Leahy, I wondered what his next decision would be. I wouldn't be around to find out.

I went below to eat my breakfast and tidy the galley. I checked in the forward cabin; it looked like they had taken their things and otherwise left it as it was. Leahy remembered to take his extra cigarettes from behind the cabin door. I guess now I would really have to quit.

I spent the rest of the morning making adjustments to my sails while I waited for the afternoon trades to come up. I practiced hauling up the throat and peak halyards together; I measured off lengths on the corresponding downhaul and marked them with whippings in brown twine. It was a solo sailor's trick to help find the proper length to tie off in a pinch without having to test it each time. That's what I was now: a solo sailor.

Later I would go by the harbor master's office and let them know of my intention to sail. And see if any complaints were filed against me. I laughed again. The tension had left. I was eager to move on with the *Gracias*. It was just her and I now. She was a fine ship, and a good companion. I trusted her for whatever came next. We would cross the Pacific together. I would take good care of her, and in turn, I knew she would take care of me. I wasn't worried about this part of my crew.

PART III

CHAPTER TWENTY-TWO

April 14, 1962
Location: 15° 42' 16" N
              150° 0' 30" W

The world looked like a bowl was set over it, capturing all the light. The sky, in every direction, was a pale, clear pink. Clouds trimmed the horizon in the far, far distance. Around the *Gracias* the ocean was the steel-blue of early morning. Here we were, just a small slab of wood and sail, out on this vast sea. As the sun rose, the sky turned lighter, almost white. Streaks of goldenrod shone in the eastern sky. And shortly an orange ball appeared, casting its glow across the horizon and shaming all the previous beautiful, delicate colors in its boldness. The sun was up.

I eased my way back below, careful not to bump my shoulder in the narrow companionway. Each morning when I first woke it felt as stiff as if it were set in concrete. As I moved about it warmed up slowly. It still hurt like hell.

According to the marks on my chart, I had been at sea nineteen days. My time in and out of the doldrums had held me back. I was making no records here. If I was lucky, and if the *Gracias* was where I thought, I should be seeing land today or tomorrow. After breakfast I adjusted the sails and hoped to ease into a good pace for the day.

We moved along at six to eight knots most of the morning. At noon I trimmed the sails and prepared to climb the mast. I was eager to go aloft and take another sighting. This time I took every precaution.

My safety harness was tied around my waist with a long line connecting me to the base of the mast below. The *Gracias* and I would not be separated. Double-checking the pulleys, I got in position. With my binoculars hanging from my neck, I slowly cranked my way up the mast. Hand over hand, a few inches at a time, I pulled myself up. My shoulder burned in agony every time I used my left arm. I stayed with it. Almost there. Near the top I made the pulley line secure with two knots and steadied myself. I took a deep breath. My hands were clammy and sweat was beading on my forehead.

"Let's take a looksee," I said to the sky, to the mast, to the *Gracias*. I looked through the binoculars, first to the northwest. In those round circles I saw more silver-gray sea, dropping off into the horizon. The end of the world. There it was again. I checked the sun and adjusted my sights. I looked again. Just water. Was there anything else out there? I rotated to the left, looking due west now. Nothing. I put my bare foot against the mast, pushing off a bit to propel myself around some more. Due south, over the vast distance toward Tahiti. And if you miscalculated and passed those isles, you were on a long, slow drift to Antarctica. I saw nothing there.

Turning east I knew it was unlikely that I would see a shoreline. Instead, I hoped for a ship, a vessel of any kind.

Perhaps it would be a grand yacht, with a distinguished captain at the helm. The wind would blow through his long sun-bleached hair as he sipped from a noontime martini.

He would have the stature of one of the affluent homeowners who sailed on the bay near Kings Point, but with the lightness of heart and spirit that such a Pacific journey renders. He would call me over the radio and invite me to join him on deck. With his cosmopolitan air he would encourage me to share my many tales of international travel and, most recently, stories of life alone at sea. After a dinner of steaks and lobster prepared by his cheerful Jamaican crew, we would retire to the lounge with fine scotch over ice and smoke cigars and discuss celestial navigation and Greek mythology.

Or maybe it would be a large cargo ship, slow and loaded down with bananas from Central America. I would be invited to join their Spanish-speaking crew in the mess, and after saying a quick prayer, ending with *"por favor, danos buena suerte,"* in deference to their unlucky cargo, we would enjoy a hot stew of pork *picadillo* with a pile of fried cassava cooling on a greasy plate beside it. We'd play cards afterward, poker, if they had just been paid, or, if not, cribbage, the favorite game of seamen around the world. A bottle of rum would be passed around and jovial laughs would be had as the game progressed past midnight. Later, the night watchman, the bright-orange tip of his cigarette placing him at the rail, would watch me with envy as I climbed down the rope ladder to the *Gracias*. He wished he could join me and escape the ship, home, and workplace that had somehow over time become his prison. I would give him a blind salute in the dark, and motor the *Gracias* away from their small world on the water.

But the seas to the east were clear as well. It was only a great, flat expanse as far as I could see.

I let the binoculars hang from my neck and swept the back of my hand across my forehead, clearing away the sweat. There was only one more direction to look. I blinked a few times, refocusing my eyes. Any vessels to the north would likely be moving away, following the current I was working with. I lifted the binoculars to look again. There was the great sea. It seemed to pull and roll away from me. Off it went, to its very distant destination, to crash against the cold rocks and buttresses of the Alaska shoreline. The water grew colder and richer as it went. Three thousand miles away, the sea was much different. No more of this clear, beautiful, yet nearly barren South Pacific water. There, it was rich with plankton, feeding the little fish that fed the bigger fish. I sighed to myself. Regardless of what was in the water, it appeared there was nothing on it. I was alone for miles in every direction. And worse, there was no sign of land.

I came down from the mast. Going below I consulted my charts again. I took some comfort in the neat row of x's showing our progress. Some were closer together than others, yes. And some strayed a bit off course. But look at that day! April 2nd! We moved almost a whole inch! I remembered it with pride. The longest part of the journey lay behind us, we had traveled over 3,000 nautical miles. Just me and my little ship. It was hard to imagine. I had never planned to make this long excursion alone. Yet here I was, almost having done it. Success was near at hand. Any day now.

The next morning while the sea was still quiet I eagerly climbed the mast before the sun was fully up. I was still moving slowly in deference to my shoulder, but I was excited to see what was out there. I figured we were close now; land should be within sight, clearly visible, even in the twilight of dawn. I adjusted my binoculars and looked northwest. Nothing but ocean. I did a light sweep to the right, further north. Nothing. No distant volcanic mountaintop rising from the sea. No splash of water against an outlying reef or atoll. I didn't see any birds, or driftwood either. It was the same all the way around. I couldn't believe it.

The wind picked up as I ate breakfast. The sails needed adjusting. I should get to it. But it seemed like a useless exercise. Would I wake up tomorrow and still see no land? Was I making any progress at all? I was a hamster in a wheel, doing everything I could to move forward but stuck in one place.

Yet what other choice did I have? I had to do the same as yesterday, and all the days before. I had to put forth the effort, even if I didn't see the effect. After eating, I adjusted the sails; they caught a bit of wind. We settled in to a slow pace, maybe three knots. I couldn't sense if we were moving forward or just bobbing up and down.

At noon I decided to climb the mast again. Now I was keeping the bolson attached, strapped down at the base of the mast. I untied it and slipped the straps around my legs. After checking my seat, I slowly pulled myself up.

One hand on the mast to stop my swaying, I lifted the binoculars with the other. I started with that long look to the north, to the faraway shores of Alaska. Water. I swung west. More water. What a disappointing day. Not paying attention to what I was doing, I loosened the line before I was ready and made a jolting drop a quick six feet down the mast. That woke me up, and pained my already injured shoulder. "Don't get lazy, Kenny," I scolded myself. I didn't need to go through that again. Almost worse than the doldrums, it was a slow, boring day. I had to remain steadfast in my focus. I eased the rest of the way down.

Battling the wind and rain seemed preferable to enjoying the tranquil view with this slowpoke pace. My body was taut with energy. It needed somewhere to go. I felt ready to explode. There was nowhere to put it, there was nothing to fight. I stood at the helm, blindly looking off into the distance. All that flat sea ahead. My eyes began to glaze over. It didn't matter. There was no danger of running into anything.

The sails drooped above. I should adjust a few degrees port. I cranked the winch and the boom moved over. The mainsail stiffened a bit, and then drooped, looking worse than before. Maybe back the other way. I cranked the winch back in the opposite direction, giving it an extra turn. The boom slid back, and over a few degrees. The sail almost held up. Was there more wind here?

Looking in the distance I thought I saw a glimpse of white water; wind blowing off the tops of waves. I should adjust the sail again. Give it more starboard. The boom swung a few degrees. The sail sagged. Where was this wind I was seeing? Maybe we should turn a bit. I adjusted the tiller. Looking up at the sail I couldn't tell if it was any different than when I first started. I corrected again.

I don't know how long I chased the wind this way. My body felt numb. Ruled by my restless mind I moved about in a heated daze. More starboard, more port, and back again. The *Gracias* was moving helter-skelter under my poor command. I only noticed when the winch handle began to slip from my grasp, slick with my own sweat. The wind had fallen completely. It was time to stop.

I took a deep breath. Forcing it never worked. I went below deck.

In the salon I looked at my bookshelf. Here I had some of the finest works of seaman from around the globe. I had Eric Hiscock's *Voyaging Under Sail*, and of course Slocum's *Sailing Alone Around the World*. In addition, there were books that appeared more useful with their thick, dark blue spines. *The Ashley Book of Knots*, *The American Practical Navigator*, the

Abridged Nautical Almanac, and a copy of *The Ship's Medicine Chest and First Aid at Sea* I had picked up somewhere. But, truly, I enjoyed the more anecdotal works of Hiscock and Slocum. In particular, Hiscock provided much nautical explanation and posed problems for debate, citing reputable sources and including his strong opinion, mostly based on experience. Every well-trained sailor enjoys a debate like this. We were well-practiced in our Kings Point days.

The Nickel was a dive bar close to campus. We spent many of those, and many late hours there. Our favorite booth was in the far back corner. Worn red vinyl cushions lined the seats and the varnished wood table was engraved with names, initials, and petroglyph-like artwork. From this corner we could watch Queens' truck drivers and longshoremen come and go. It was usually BJ, Cy Kepler, and I; most of our classmates who lived nearby went home Saturday afternoons. We would spend the evening rehashing our morning regatta with the Windjammers. We discussed the competition, the conditions, and our own performances.

"You were moving out great, Kepler, until you looked back to wave at your girl there on the pier. One little rough crest and you were broaching to!" BJ teased him. It had been an especially close race that morning.

Cy laughed. "It wasn't that! The wind had picked up. I didn't make a turn, I was trying to adjust five degrees."

"Well, that five degrees cost you the race!" I laughed, then tried to be helpful. "You could have heeled port instead. I saw the Webb team do that last week. It looked like a good strategy."

"True enough."

"Or, what I would have done is heeled steeper. You could have cleared at least twenty degrees, and made more use of that lift."

"Good point. If I didn't want to swamp her on the high seas!" Cy laughed at his joke. The Long Island Sound was far from the high seas, especially on a gentle spring morning. "Anyway, I'll take second place. It still gives us points for the team."

"Whatdaya think, Maggie, should he have heeled in that last bit?" I asked our waitress as she set down another pitcher of beer. Maggie was a petite, capable, green-eyed, dark-haired beauty. She was studying design at the Fashion Institute of Technology. Raised in Kansas City, she held her own with the greasy crowd at the Nickel, but I think she liked us soft, out-of-town scholarly boys.

"Sure, whatever you say, Captain!" Maggie gave me a quick wink as she turned away. She called us all Captain, which pleased us to no end, considering it was a title none of us had earned yet. Cy gave me an elbow in the ribs. "There's something you should take a sail on!"

"Ha! Yeah, sure." She also winked at all of us, so I tried not to take it personally.

"You getting this one, Bohlin? I think you owe from the last round," Cy said.

"You know I'd rather owe it to you than cheat you out of it."

"You always say that."

"It's always true!" I laughed at my own joke and pulled out my wallet.

I wished those fellows were with me now. BJ would be good company with his sailing stories. I was in the middle of the Pacific Ocean, thousands of miles from any bar, but for old times' sake I poured myself a finger of whisky.

Throwing it down, I poured another, and looked for a good passage in *Voyaging Under Sail* to debate with Hiscock. Here was a gem:

> *"It is obvious that as the luff rope rolls down on top of itself, and the leech rope rolls down in a spiral, the after end of the boom must be increased in diameter if it is not to droop as the reef is rolled in."*

Well of course, *obviously*. But, as was his way, Hiscock had another point to make, and, as usual, another source to cite:

> *"But that is not the only consideration, for as the late Claud Worth pointed out in 'Yacht Cruising' many years ago, the boom requires an even greater diameter in the middle, otherwise when reefed the sail will have too much belly."*

He went on to describe how to temporarily adjust your boom thickness, and specifically the taper, until you have the right shape so as not to have too much belly. It was all quite fascinating, really. This guy knew his stuff. I poured another length of whisky in my glass. While my instructors at Kings Point were all top notch, nothing can compare to the real experience of a sailor putting theory to practice. Here I was, doing the same. Perhaps I should be making some notes to submit to Hiscock upon my return to civilization. I read on.

I woke on the bench in the salon. Arms hanging over one side, my face stuffed into the bench's cushion. I untwisted from that position and sat up. Whoa. In that movement, it felt like a wrecking ball had swung across the inside of my head, from one side to the other and back. I steadied myself against the bench, lest it have momentum and try to swing again. Ah. It stopped. It felt good to sit still.

My mouth felt like it was stuffed with newspapers that had sat in a barn all summer. Dry, dusty, and rough in my throat. I leaned forward and stood, putting a hand on the edge of the counter to steady myself, and made my way to the water container. I poured some into a glass I found in the sink. Only when I brought it to my face did I smell the whisky still there. I drank it anyway, cringing at the brief smell, like gasoline fumes escaping the tank before the lid is screwed tight. I poured myself another, and drank it too. OK. That was better. Where had I left that aspirin? First, I wanted to go above board and see how things looked outside.

I put my hand above my eyes to shield them from the bright light. It was blazing out there. The sun was high above, almost noon, I suspected. I had slept through the night. I took a deep breath of salt air. The wind was brisk: I might be able to make some progress today.

Moving lightly about the deck, careful not to cause much jolting to my head, I slowly, precariously prepared the sails. The mainsail unfurled with a large "whack!" sound, reverberating through my head like a slap in the face. I slowly moved to the helm, where I found a bit of shade.

I consulted my compass, and turned her west. The sails fluttered, making a warping noise that seemed to bounce back and forth between my temples. I took another deep breath and held still for a moment. I locked the tiller and moved forward to trim the sails a bit. That reduced the flutter and we began a nice easy sail, over nearly flat water, maybe moving seven to eight knots.

Since everything seemed to be smooth sailing, after a breakfast of chicken noodle soup I decided to go back to Hiscock's book and pick up where I'd left off. Sitting still for a while was appealing. I went behind the helm and leaned back against the transom. It was a fine place to read, and soon I was lost deep in a debate about the benefits and drawbacks of the square sail.

CHAPTER TWENTY-THREE

April 16, 1962
Location: 15° 43' 16" N
            150° 05' 30" W

After some time I noticed the pages of my book became dim; I looked to the sky and saw it had faded from a clear, sunny blue, to a barren white. Little puffs of clouds were all around, blocking out the sun. These began to darken as I watched. A squall was coming. I stood up. To the east a dark charcoal-gray wall of clouds loomed. The bottom of the wall was a perfect flat line; the water below it shimmered in silver. It was raining there, and it was coming my way.

My head was still feeling a dull, low throb, like the very slow motor of a dinghy navigating along the shoreline. This squall looked wetter than the last. Slowly, carefully, in the rising pitch, I made my way around deck, ensuring lines were tied off properly, and if not necessary, put in storage lockers. I reefed the foresail and the main, and doused the jib, taking it down completely. I closed all hatches securely.

Looking aft, I saw the storm was closer. Now the wall of gray had lengthened over the horizon and darker round bulges formed along its bottom edge like fat waterskins, ready to burst. It looked foreboding. I turned on my mast light as well as my bow and stern lanterns. There was an eerie rattle in the rigging as the *Gracias* began to toss roughly. Waves were coming up at over twelve feet, at my best estimate. Water was sloshing on the deck and blowing in the wind. We were still only feeling the edges of the storm; I knew within the hour it would change drastically. I decided to eat supper while I had a chance.

Digging among the array of cans in the galley bin, I found a reassuring rectangle of Spam. This seemed like a good choice; it wouldn't splash out of a bowl. It took me a minute to work the can opener around the rim as the boat jerked up and down. I sliced it and threw it in the frying pan. The little net basket that was once full of fruit still held a single tangerine. It swung severely with the roll of the *Gracias*, hitting the wall behind it with a solid bump, like a tennis ball dribbled on a clay court. I decided to put the net away and put the tangerine out of its misery.

I ate my fried Spam standing at the stove, with a wide stance and my knees bent to catch the rough roll of the ship. I ate straight out of the frying pan, blowing on each forkful to cool it before stuffing it into my mouth. When I was finished, I washed the pan, dried it, and stowed it securely under the counter.

I put on my foul-weather gear and life jacket. I climbed through the forward hatch and stepped on deck. It was completely black here, save for the *Gracias'* night lanterns. The looming clouds had moved over us and rain was falling. Barefoot, I made my way toward the bow. Unless we were in a heavy sou'wester, I preferred the grip of my own feet. We were pitching heavily, the bow diving down into the troughs of each wave with a heavy fall. Spray came flying onto the deck. The waves had grown to over twenty feet. I kneeled at the storage chest at the front and cautiously pried it open. Careful to keep the lid low and not let any water in, I pawed through my gear until my hand wrapped around the nylon straps of my safety harness. Better safe than sorry. Securing the hatch, I stood and put the harness around my waist. Carefully judging the timing of the roll of the next wave, I took one quick, long step across the deck to the starboard rail and held on to it as I moved aft. Here I clipped my harness to the jackline. With that quick snap the *Gracias'* destiny and mine were bound together. If she rolled over, so would I. I was hoping it wouldn't come to that. "When you have the chance to do it right, do it." These words popped into my head like a mantra. If there was anything they drilled into us at Kings Point, it was this: don't put yourself in a position where later you wish you had done things differently.

As such, my best plan was to heave to. This was not a night to work the wind. We were in hard seas and my aim was to steer the *Gracias* to keep her at an even keel. My only goal was to keep her upright. I had become used to her sure roll and easy demeanor. Feeling her tossed about the waves like a little yellow rubber duck in a gigantic ogre's bathtub was unnerving. My palms were wet with saltwater and sweat. I took a deep breath and tried to calm my rushing pulse.

I went to the masts and doused both remaining sails. Waves were now crashing across the beam and splashing at my feet; saltwater stung my eyes. I tried to duck my head and protect them as I quickly bundled the sails and made the ties secure.

We climbed the face of each wave coming toward us, and crashed down hard on the other side. It would only get worse if the wind got stronger. I went aft and pulled my sea anchor from its storage chest. I attached a length of chain to add to the weight of it, to help it sink squarely. Water washed over my hands as I secured the anchor's line to a bitt on deck. Straightening up, the wind whipped at my face and pellets of rain smacked my skin. Holding the bulk of the yellow fabric of the sea anchor in my hands, I stood at the transom, looking toward the bow. The head rail pitched upwards, going up the next wave. As she crossed the top, flat for a moment, just before she pitched down, I tossed the anchor with all my might. It flew off into the next crest behind us, rising with the water for a moment, before the chain brought it down. This was good positioning relative to the motion of the *Gracias*. I saw a yellow-white flutter in the water. It moved further and further back as it caught the current. At twenty yards away the line went taut; the anchor sank a bit, now a pale blur under the dark sea.

The *Gracias* lurched hard one more time, and then seemed to ease into a better routine with the waves. This, at least, would help reduce the pitching. If I kept her steady, bearing directly into the waves, we shouldn't have much roll either. This is what I hoped as I took the helm.

The wind howled, blowing rain and saltwater across the aft deck, across my face. I couldn't distinguish between the two. Keeping my eyes focused on the sea before us, I watched as waves kept coming forth, seeming taller and taller. In the stark light of the forward lantern I held my breath as the bow rose up the face of each wave, up, up, up she went, plowing through the black mountain of water, pitching upward, and just as it seemed the wave would break across her, she made her way clear of the top. We were aloft, level for the briefest moment, like being at the peak of a rollercoaster, then we were pitching back down, straight into the black sea, and I held my breath again, worried that her bow would plunge into the trough and sink the whole of us. As she made clear of each watery trench and started the upward climb again, I took the quickest breath before holding it again as we went through the ride once more.

I considered adjusting my bearings and putting her at a forty-five-degree angle to the surges to reduce the heaving. But with waves this size, it was a risk. There would be a constant wash over the deck from the tops of the waves. One big one might take us over. I stayed facing them dead on.

We climbed and dropped, climbed and dropped. Ahead of me only black waves, troughs, and waves again. The monotony of climbing each wave was tiring and reassuring at the same time. "Same as the last," I assessed. The storm, while not abating, was not getting worse.

The *Gracias* seemed to hold her own plowing through the waves, I was proud of her handling in the storm. Yet, as the hours wore on, I wondered about her captain. I was very alert, tense, and cold; exhaustion made me want to crawl into a cozy corner and sleep a fortnight. My quick meal of Spam and tangerine was hours ago; my belly felt like an empty barrel, cavernous and echoing with hunger pangs. I should have thought to make some peanut butter and jelly sandwiches, and stashed them at the helm for the long haul. One of those things I had wished I'd done differently.

Rain and saltwater splashed on to my hand, tightly gripped on the tiller, and crept down my sleeve, soaking the sweatshirt I wore beneath. While it was no New England winter, my face was freezing. My feet were ghostly white, cold, almost numb. Periodically I moved up and down in low squats, trying to warm my legs. I was afraid I'd lose all feeling there. What if I couldn't stand at the helm?

Adrenaline coursed through me in a slow undercurrent. My senses were completely tuned in to the nature around me; the dark face of each wave, the churning current below us, splashes across the deck, the wind and rain in my face. On this thin line of electric current I stayed standing through the night.

A meager dawn came, lighting the sky from black to gray. But visibility was still poor; rain came down hard and fast, making the day a long, eternal twilight. I stayed at the helm, helping guide the *Gracias* straight over another wave, and another, and another.

A movement caught my eye. It wasn't on the water, but closer. Something was on the deck with me. My vision was a lazy blur after so many hours of looking off into the distance. I blinked and tried to focus.

My father sat on the portside aft locker. He was reading a newspaper, holding the pages out before him in the dim light, oblivious to the wind and rain. His glasses were streaked with raindrops, but he continued to look down at the wet, gray sheets, engrossed in his reading.

"Dad!" My mouth was parched, my throat hoarse. My words came out soft and dry. I swallowed and tried again.

"Hey! Dad!" He didn't look up.

"Dad! Could you come here?" Couldn't he see me here? "I could really use a hand." My words whipped away in the wind. I yelled again.

"Dad! Look at me! Dad?" My eyes warmed, tears slid down my cheeks. He was right there, why didn't he help me?

He turned a page in the paper.

"Dad! Don't you see me?!?" My throat was swollen with a lump; my nose running. I wiped it with the back of my hand. "Dad?" Seeing him right there before me, I yearned to hear his voice, to know he was real.

Without looking at me, he said, "It's all right, Kenny, weatherman says it'll clear up tomorrow. You'll still be able to go on your Scout's camping trip." He neatly folded the paper, tucked his reading glasses into his breast pocket, and stood, looking off into the distance.

"Call me when it's time for supper." He walked to the hatch and made his way down the companionway, tall and composed, as easily as if he were walking down his own front steps.

I shook my head. Had he just been here? My father? On the *Gracias* with me? I could have reached out to touch him. The man whose strict rules had been a reassuring constant in my childhood. He walked with the natural ease of his long legs, the same stride I had known my whole life. The pitch of the boat didn't move him at all. I heard his voice, clear and sure, even if he couldn't hear me. It was him. But how could he be here?

The heat surrounded me like I was in an oven. It was getting hotter and hotter. I began to sweat. I had to escape to save myself before I exploded in the heat. I couldn't see anything but a pale glow before me. Had I been blinded? What was happening? I was bound and couldn't move. Had I been captured? Was I in the brig of an enemy ship?

"Wake up, Kenny! Wake up!" My own voice echoed in my head, demanding. It seemed as if my life depended on following its orders. "Open your eyes!" My eyes. Slowly I opened them a bit. The light was dim but the glow of it was startling. My lashes were crusty, the skin around my eyes stiff. I rubbed them clear. Salt peeled away and rolled down my cheeks in crumbs. I was still hot. I looked down at my arm and legs. Still in the yellow slicker and pants of my foul-weather gear, it was like being inside a sauna. Undoing the snaps I got hung up around the waist; lo, the safety harness was still around me. I unclipped it. Jacket off, I stood, wobbly, and found my legs.

The sea was flat, a dull gray all around me. The storm had passed. The sun shone somewhere above through a light gauzy patch of clouds. I tried to get my bearings. I was here. Here aboard the *Gracias*. We were at sea in the Pacific. There had been a storm. I had survived. I conquered those monstrous, terrifying waves. Thousands of waves. I had faced them, every one. I had beaten the storm. I tried to rally some pride around it, but it was an empty win, celebrated alone, deflated and exhausted. I eased onto a locker to sit for a moment and look at the gray sea.

I no longer knew what day it was. I hadn't marked the ship's log today. What about yesterday? Two, three days ago? I couldn't recall. The detailed notes I'd taken at first were useless now. I had seen no sign of life or land for weeks. There was a chance we were on our way to Alaska. Or perhaps the tides had turned and I was headed back toward the Marquesas. The storm had left me lost in this great sea.

No one on Earth knew where I was or where I was headed. How would anyone know to miss me if I didn't make my destination? They wouldn't send a rescue party.

If no one missed me, did I matter, in the great scheme of this planet, this universe? Was a single person out there thinking of me? Hoping I was safe and sound? Wondering what had become of me? Like the philosophical tree in the woods, would anyone notice if I fell? If there was no one there to notice, did I even exist at all? I had survived the storm, but so what? I was alone in this sea and on this planet. Alone in the great, wide universe.

I hadn't set the sails or adjusted the rudder, and the current kept moving the boat along. I was content with that. I had no friends or family wondering what was holding me up. There was no captain barking orders at me. I could do as I pleased.

In this mood, I stripped off the rest of my wet clothing, left it in a lump on deck, and climbed down the ladder for my bunk. Wherever we were, it didn't matter. Sorry, *Gracias*, you are on your own. If we drifted for days it wouldn't make a difference; no one was waiting to receive us on the other side of the ocean. I wrapped my salty, damp body in my blankets and let my fate go to the currents.

CHAPTER TWENTY-FOUR

Date: April ? 1962
Location: Unknown

The painful growl of my empty stomach pushed me out of my bunk late the next morning. Finding a still sea, I set my line, lay belly down on the deck, and watched the water. Was I in the doldrums again, or was there just no wind today? What did it matter? We were becalmed either way.

The floater bobbed lightly on the flat sea. It moved on the invisible power that began with a bit of wind, somewhere far off in the east, and continued to move through the waves across great fetches of sea. The water itself never traveled significantly, but the illusion of it moving was due to this energy. This force creates the waves, currents, and tides. It moves whether we know it or not, whether we chose to recognize it or not, day and night. While babies are born, while a man harvests wheat from a field, while a racehorse passes the winning post. It moves while we work and sleep, regardless of the conditions of mankind. Through all of eternity, before, now, and forever. It moves through great expanses, through all aspects of our entire planet, our atmosphere, space and beyond. It is a ceaseless, silent interchange.

It was our second year at Kings Point, and now I had Lieutenant Carney as an instructor in Seamanship Lab. With his characteristically dramatic arched eyebrows and bulging eyes, he explained the magical energy of the sea.

"You see, gentlemen, Newton's laws of physics hold true, in all circumstances, including weather at sea. What's one of those laws?" he asked the class.

"Sir, every action causes an equal and opposite reaction, sir," called out a midshipman near the back.

"OK, yes, that's one of them. In the case of oceans, a good example is the seismic sea wave, or tsunami. When the Earth moves, perhaps by an earthquake, or maybe a volcanic eruption, it causes a force of energy. This energy creates waves in the water, and depending on the strength of the initial force, these waves, or really, the energy within the waves, can carry over great fetches of sea, thousands of miles. Now this energy in itself is not harmful. Nor is the water as it moves in waves across the ocean. But it needs somewhere to go, they both do. As the energy approaches land, it slows, causing a backup, if you will, of the energy, and in this case, the water, which piles up and eventually breaks, in what we call the tidal wave.

"What's another one of Newton's laws?"

"Sir, inertia, sir. Every object in a state of motion, or rest, remains in that state unless an external force is applied, sir," I answered. It was one of my favorites. The first time I heard this in high school physics I pictured the lazy dairy cows at Fritz Anderson's farm. It took a lot of external force to make one of them take a lethargic step.

"Good. External forces. Here we get to talk about one of the more interesting weather phenomena: the hurricane.

As you know, there is a constant exchange between the sea and atmosphere." He turned to the blackboard and drew a flat line, presumably the sea.

"In the most basic terms: under the right conditions, as moist air is drawn into the atmosphere from the ocean, it cools, and condensation occurs." Here he tapped a bunch of dots onto the board, to indicate droplets of water.

"The act of cooling causes a latent heat that is thusly released and warms the air. As we know, heat rises." He drew an arrow up from the ocean through the dots of moisture. "The cooler air here"—he sketched vertical lines on either side of the dots—"creates a form of an upright tunnel. In the case of creating a hurricane, the warmer air rises, constricted within this tunnel." He made a spiraling line up from the ocean, between the vertical lines and through the dots.

"Once it exits the tunnel, it spreads outward, moving in a clockwise fashion. It continues to draw more warm air and moisture to it. The moisture acts as fuel, moving the winds faster and stronger, making the hurricane bigger, stronger, more forceful." He made several large circles on the board, leaving off with a dramatic flourish, just for fun.

"With this example, we can see how Newton's law plays out. What state of motion are we looking at with these objects? Where does an external force come in?"

From the safe vantage point of the utopian life at Kings Point, New York, it was fun to sit in the classroom and have theoretical discussions, observe weather diagrams, and picture the rising winds and the growing, perfect cylindrical shape of a hurricane. It was a good discussion, and an important thing to learn. But on the water it was different.

After a time at sea, a sailor needs no diagrams. He learns the feel of exchanges, and can tell when the winds and temperatures are right to bring about a storm. Asleep in his berth, his ears can detect a change in the way the current slaps the hull. He quickly adapts to his role out here; the wind is there to be caught, to move us forward. The clouds to bring us rain. The moon to pull the tides, and the stars to be read, to guide our way. A well-trained sailor has everything he needs at his disposal. With this eternal source of energy here for us, nothing is impossible. It is the energy exchange that makes life—the quiet, sly, brilliant, all-present form of life that perfectly runs our universe. He plans his rigging and sets his sails with will and determination, all the while knowing he must consider the will of the wind and currents as well.

I knew these things to be true; but I was losing faith in my ability to work with what I had. The wind was not cooperating. I wasn't sure where I was, and more so, didn't know if I could rely on my past reckonings. After all, they had put me here. If the universe runs so perfectly, why was I stuck on this flat sea, lost and alone?

CHAPTER TWENTY-FIVE

Date: April ? 1962
Location: Unknown

I was lonely beyond anything I imagined possible. My body was hollow; each breath seemed to ricochet through the emptiness. I was just a shell of a man, out here alone, with no human or creature to validate my small, petty existence. A dark feeling hung inside me. It wasn't fear or sadness; it was merely the brink of these, like storm clouds gathering, about to spill over. I was desperate to escape them. I knew this storm, I'd felt it during those deeply homesick days in the Navy; and, longer ago, deep in the folds of my memory, over the winter I longed for my mother's return. I tried to turn my mind away from the sadness, but soon tears wet my eyes. It was happening: the storm was breaking. It was a plummeting emptiness that obliterated my body; I felt only my tears and my stuffy nose. Everything else had floated away.

I was a sad, soggy mess. Like a little baby. How embarrassing.

It was better to be alone anyway, I told myself. If I'd had some mates aboard, I wouldn't want them to see this. Or see the madness they themselves held. In close quarters men can become irritable. If any are unhappy types ashore, you can guarantee they will be twice as salty at sea. They can be unpredictable. If they are tired of eating canned soup every meal. If the sun shone too hot that day. If someone beat them badly at cribbage. They were worse than women. And if they were drinking, watch out. There was a time aboard the *Alamar* when everything went to hell with the flip of a card.

"Raise." O'Malley put in a stack of chips. It was down to him and Ryan, they were head to head. On the flop we saw a pair of queens, both red, and a six of hearts. Ryan met his raise, and nodded at Chuckie, the dealer.

"All good?" Chuckie asked.

"Yep."

He took the top card off the pile, placed it to the side, and dropped the fourth, another six, diamonds.

Ryan tapped the table. "Good."

O'Malley raised again, this time with a taller stack.

Ryan matched his chips.

"We good?" Chuckie asked.

"Yep."

Now the table was laid with two pairs, all red.

Chuckie discarded the top card, and put down the last. They were at the river. Jack of hearts.

O'Malley pushed the last of his chips forward into the disjointed pot in the middle of the table.

Ryan counted out what was left of his.

"Go ahead, whatever you got. I'm not a picky winner."

He arched a dark Irish eyebrow toward O'Malley.

"OK. Let's see."

He had a queen of spades and an ace.

"Full house!" O'Malley laughed with a hearty he he he he he. True. He had three queens and two sixes.

Ryan smiled.

"Nice." He turned over his cards. "But I have a flush."

Indeed, he had a two of hearts and a ten, also of hearts. Whatever possessed him to stay in the game with those cards, I'd never guess. I suppose he was waiting for a moment like this.

"Ha!" Bowman laughed beside him. "Nice one, Ryan!"

Ryan started to pull in the chips toward him.

"Hold on a second, sailor! A full house beats a flush, everyone knows that," said O'Malley.

"What? Maybe back in Boston. But the rest of the civilized world knows a flush tops a full house. Am I right, boys?"

Heads around him shook "no."

"That's my pot, keep your greasy hands off it!"

O'Malley lunged across the table, his long black beard grazing the chips as he reached out to pull the pot to him.

"What are you doing? That's mine!"

"No it's not!"

"You're crazy!"

I knew what was going to happen next. I took a quick step back from the table.

Ryan threw a cross cut across the table, straight into O'Malley's nose. O'Malley pitched back and when he straightened up blood streamed through his mustache and into his beard. He touched his nose tentatively with his hand, and pulled it away to see blood on his fingertips.

"You bastard!"

He flew around the table and gave Ryan a strong shove. Ryan flew back, hitting the wall next to me with a hard, flat smack.

"That pot is mine, fair and square!"

He went for Ryan again, and at this point we knew it was time to step in. They had each gotten in a good wallop, diffusing some stress and the desperate loneliness of life at sea. I went to O'Malley and grabbed him by the shoulders, pulling him away from Ryan. Cassidy stepped in front of Ryan, blocking him with his boxy body.

"Cool it, men. Come on, Ryan, we all know it's O'Malley's pot. Relax." I took a towel from the counter, and sat O'Malley on the bench where I blotted the blood out of his beard.

The chips were being gathered up and stacked back in their case. There was no need to count them. Ryan didn't owe O'Malley anything. There was no cash to back our games. It was all in fun. And pride. And mad competition.

Ryan, dizzy with a near concussion, sat at the other end of the bench. He looked at the floor, bent over, still catching his breath.

O'Malley gave him a hard look. "What's your problem, Ryan? It's just cards. You need to relax. Or go take a long walk on a short pier!"

At this idea I suppressed a giggle. We were off the coast of Argentina, days away from any pier. O'Malley's half-hearted jab fell through the room like a dead bird from the sky. Cassidy chuckled. Chuckie laughed a loud "ha!" and then, finally, Ryan started to quiver on the bench. Still bent over, his shoulders shook. He slapped his knee. And when he came up, he tossed his head back, laughing like a wild man.

"Take a long walk? On a short pier? Ha ha ha ha ha! What pier? We're in the middle of nowhere! Ha! Maybe you meant a gangplank?" He laughed harder at his own joke. O'Malley laughed too, all the tension gone, just the silliness of the night left among us.

My tears stopped, I wiped my drippy nose on my shirtsleeve. A game of cards with the crew sounded like fun. I didn't have a crew, but I did have cards. And a game. Tucked on the bookshelf at the end of the row, held in by the little keeper rail, was the cribbage board I made during my last visit home.

My father had found a pretty piece of cherry in his scrap wood. It was cut straight through the trunk and still had bits of bark around the edges, yet it had an odd triangular shape. With three sides I thought, "this must be meant for use for three" and the image of a three-man cribbage board came to mind. I drilled the holes and gave it a sanding and nice varnish. BJ, Jean, and I had made good use of this three-person board, making up rules for three players, and playing many late nights as we kept each other company on watch.

Here it was before me on the shelf. A small piece of New England forest had made it halfway across the Pacific with me aboard the *Gracias*. The rings of the tree were still visible. Fine brown lines moved out from the middle like ripples on a pond. I traced my finger over them, counting. Twenty-six. We were the same age.

I poured out the slim finish nails I had painted red, black, and white for markers, and set it on the mess table. I would deal a round and see how it went, playing all three hands.

I tried to be completely random and arbitrary when I tossed a card from each hand into the crib. That proved hard; my mind went straight to making points. Next round I resolved to do it blind, cards face down. As I continued on, I found it was easy to plan each play and make points as I knew which card was the most useful to play next. I resigned myself to that fact; someone had to be the winner, didn't they? It may as well be me.

This made for boring, predictable play. I decided to liven it up with a bit of whiskey. I found a glass among the dirty dishes piled in the sink. I poured myself a long drink, and continued on.

"Ha! Still ahead of the pack!" I exclaimed after four or five hands. I had the advantage here. The sound of my voice, the first time I'd used it in days, was rough and strained. I hadn't had a conversation in weeks.

My vision blurred. I couldn't make out my cards. It wasn't the whisky. The tears had returned.

It wasn't supposed to be this way.

BJ and I had planned this trip from our earliest days at Kings Point. It was to be the two of us, maybe a couple of others, on our own sailboat, seeing the world. We had worked hard to learn all we could and complete our schooling. We put in our best efforts in the Navy. We saved our money. We stayed up late nights charting our course while working on other vessels. We made a detailed itinerary with all of our planned stops. We lined up friends and family members to send ahead mail and supplies. And yet, after all of our preparation, The Worldwide Tour had failed. It was like a speeding train that flew off its tracks and over a cliff; all of its momentum, along with the futures of those on board, shot into empty space and landed in a rocky chasm with a crumpled crash. It was an enormous disappointment that sat heavy on my heart. All because of the damn depth of this keel we rode on and the equilibrium between BJ's ears. How could it be?

Continuing on without BJ and Jean, I'd had to stay focused. I hadn't expected to have to make my way through the canal with a new crew. And then trying to figure out what the hell was going on with Patty. Then giving her and

Leahy the heave-ho. And after that reconfiguring my route and making my way alone. I never wanted to do this alone. My fist hit the table, the little nails bounced and scattered. Here, on a long, lonely day at sea, I finally acknowledged the thought I'd been trying to ignore. There was no more Worldwide Tour. Our plan had failed. I had failed. It was over. I never should have started this journey to begin with. Who was I to think I could sail around the world? I grew up in a landlocked place and I should have stayed there. I should have stuck with what I knew: milking cows and baling hay. Now I was out here in the middle of nowhere. What was I going to do next? I couldn't turn around. Even if by some miracle I lived to make it to Hawaii, by no means could I go back to Leicester. My father would think me a failure. The entire town wasn't expecting me back until 1964, at the earliest. How could I face them? My face became hot and tears ran down my cheeks. I was crying like a baby again. What a loser.

I had to go on deck. I needed air.

I left the cards spewed messily across the table with my empty glass and climbed up the companionway. I went to the bow and wiped my eyes and looked around. The skies were clear and soft, a brief bit of clouds lined the horizon. It was hazy out in the far distance. I turned a full circle, taking in the entire sea. It was still there. The same as yesterday, and the day before. We might even be in the same place. For all I knew we'd drifted past Hawaii and were on our way to Japan.

CHAPTER TWENTY-SIX

Date: April ? 1962
Location: Unknown

Bits of water shone through the air, a sprinkle of drops catching the light, glimmering as they fell. Fatter drops hit the ground with loud smacks. It was a hot August day in Leicester. I was holding a hose, shooting toward Jimmy and Kathy as they ran circles around me. They laughed as the water hit them; a big splash sounded as the water slammed against Jimmy's back, soaking his T-shirt. I heard a low moan; was he hurt? Then a long sigh. I dropped the hose and ran to him. But then a splash again, this time, it was water hitting water. Water. I shot upright in my bunk.

Before I put two thoughts together I was standing in the salon, rubbing my eyes, looking at the floor. It was dry. Perhaps there was a leak in the forward cabin. I looked there, and in the head; all dry. Portholes were closed tight. I heard the splashing noise again. I quickly climbed on deck. It was near dark; the sun had retired for the evening, leaving behind a magnificent deep blue sea, and a clear pink sky that darkened to navy blue directly above. It was quiet.

I listened for the dreaded sound of water running from a hole in the hull. All was silent. I had a moment of relief.

Then, the guttural moan and a loud whoosh of air. I turned around. Off the starboard rail I saw a spray of water, like a sprinkler set out on the lawn in summer, rising up from a center point and dissipating in a wide circle. It rose almost fifteen feet; the spray blew across the deck, landing on my bare feet. It smelled like rotten fish. As the air cleared I saw its source. Not twenty feet from the *Gracias* lay a whale. It swam alongside us, its head at our bow and tail surpassing the stern. I guessed it to be almost fifty feet long. There was another loud snorting sound and a smaller expulsion of moisture this time. Its black skin had a sheen of water on it, and looked as smooth and slick as an inner tube being ridden down a river on a sunny day.

On the other side of the whale the water roiled and a series of flat ovals seemed to cover the surface. Another spray came out of the water, this one much smaller and finer. A small whine went with it, reminding me of the calves at the dairy, calling for their mothers. And, indeed, it was a calf. A smaller version of its mother, yet still bigger than a porpoise, this new creature hung close to her flank. The mother turned on her side, exposing her pectoral fin. She raised it and gave a slap on the water, and again. In this position I saw a bit of her underbelly, striped with long ridges, like a piece of corrugated aluminum, it was white and spotted with gray. Fat drops splashed up in the air, a few landed on the *Gracias'* deck.

The last of the sunlight was gone and the *Gracias* lay dark; I hadn't turned on any lanterns. Tonight the moon hung full and high. How many nights had it been since I'd last seen it? It cast a white, ethereal spotlight on the dark water. Its refection was caught in the glassiness of the whale's huge eye, pointed skyward as she continued to slap the water. Her great jaws stretched open, in a playful yawn. She seemed joyful, almost silly. Was she playing? The noise she made was like a form of Morse code. Was she communicating something to her calf with those movements, those taps? I moved toward the bow for a better vantage point. Looking over her back I saw the baby there, now turned on his side. He was slapping the water too, imitating her movement. Side by side they splashed in the night water.

I was enchanted as I watched them tap out perfect rhythms, one following the other. After a while the baby seemed to tire of the slapping and rolled to his rightful position. The mother righted herself as well and with a light blow out her blowhole, the way you might clear a snorkel, she tilted forward, submerging her gigantic head, and then her body, and made a large, glorious slap on the water with her thick, strong tail, pushing her deep into the dark water, bouncing the *Gracias* in her wake. Down she went, to what depths I would never know. The baby trailed her, his smaller tail making a little splash. I stood leaning over the rail, looking down into the black night sea searching for any trace of them below. I saw nothing but the small wash they left behind. I waited. I looked out at the dark sea, illuminated only by a streak of moonlight. They weren't there. I looked across the rigging to the port side. Nothing. Then the *Gracias* lurched with a small, almost undiscernible pull. I looked up in time to see the mama whale clear the surface with a clean jump. Powered entirely by her mighty tail, she came straight out of the water. Droplets glistened on her skin in the moonlight. She curved her body in a thick arc, and fell straight down, flat on the water, in a bold belly flop. The impact made the *Gracias* move back in the wake of ripples. Soon the calf came out of the water, in a low, flat jump that landed with a smack.

She dove down again, and again the baby followed. Her jump took her a bit higher this time, up, clearing the surface, and landing with a sloppy, silly slap that moved the sea and called out across its surface like an echo. Right behind her the baby made his leap. She went down again, and upon surfacing this time, the mama whale gave a little spin, showing her broad belly and landing with a crash on her back. The baby followed. He was mimicking her movements in the oldest form of learning among men and all creatures since before time. They went on like this for a while, leaping and diving just off the starboard rail, rocking the *Gracias* in their wakes. Their tons of flesh moved easily with just a push of their muscular tails. I was amazed.

As the *Gracias* drifted and bobbed in the moonlight, the cow stayed near, always keeping an even, measured distance with the hull. While she seemed trusting enough, she stayed between us and the calf. She kept him safe. It was the primary objective of her life—to keep him alive. She taught him what he needed to know to survive in this great sea. How to find the richest, tastiest beds of plankton; how to avoid predators; and how to make their annual migration across this huge ocean. And maybe, tonight, she was showing him how to play.

After a time the cow rolled back onto her side, slapping the water again. Her calf did so as well. They slapped and splashed, applauding their great breaching performance. Then, with one sudden, synchronized motion, they rolled back onto their bellies, and dove smoothly into the sea, leaving behind just the shimmer of the moon on their dark wake. I didn't see them again.

I let my gaze drift out over the moonlit sea.

My mother would miss me. Not that crazy lady in Florida, but my mother. The one who kept me warm and safe, the one who quietly prepared my favorite meals when she'd seen I'd had a hard day, the one who was always proud of me.

I met her on their wedding day. I was watching from the top of the staircase, tucked behind one of the strong square oak posts of the banister in Aunt Caroline's house. I looked down upon them, coming in from the brisk spring day, fresh from the courthouse. It was one of those days that sparkled; the sun shone bright, reflecting off the softening snowbanks, and silvery streams of melted snow filled the streets. Fat drops of water dripped off the edge of the roof and glistened through the window. She stood in the front room in a neat white dress suit, her brown hair pressed with curls, both hands tightly clutching a small purse. My father left her to go to the kitchen, looking for me, I supposed.

In a moment, he came back into the room and called my name up the stairs. I stood slowly, reluctant to lose my hiding place.

"There you are Kenny, come down here."

When I reached the bottom step he came to stand before me and bent down to look into my face, both hands on my shoulders. "Kenny, this is your new mother. Phyllis." He turned aside, hand still on one shoulder, and from this vantage point I took in her small plump frame, her strong hands, and her body that seemed both stiff and jittery in her plain white suit. She wore low, flat shoes and glasses. When I looked up into her round face I saw a wide smile that denied all of the plainness, and bright green-blue eyes that shone from behind her glasses. She was alight and glowing there, ready to take me in. I stepped off the bottom step and across the small entryway to her and wrapped my arms around her waist, burying my face into the stiff fabric of her suit, feeling the warmth of her soft belly beneath it. "Hi, Mama."

"Well, hello, Kenny, it's so very nice to meet you." She held me tight. There was a flutter in my heart, like when Snowball curled up in a circle on my chest and her purr shook through my body. I knew in that moment this mother would never want to leave me.

And she never did. From that instant, she was my mother in all the ways that mattered.

I imagined her sitting at the kitchen table, rereading my last telegram from Colon, and wondering what might have become of me since. I couldn't let her worry about me.

With every sunrise the world turns, whether you chose to be part of it or not. Whales swim the sea, night and day, unconcerned with your presence. A true seaman finds his place within the harmony of his world—his ship, his crew, the sea, and the heavens—to ensure the success of his journey. He is only one part of this majestic formula, founded in physics and bound by the laws of nature. The current always moves, going where it may, regardless of your preferences. You can allow yourself to drift along with it, as many do. Or you can use your will and determination to work with the current and the perfect science of nature to take you where you want to go. There is a kind of magic there, a magic that might surprise you with its reassurance that your effort is worthwhile, and your faith well placed.

Perhaps Hawaii wouldn't be so bad. The waterfront is a small place; if I knew anyone in port I would find them shortly. I could find work. It might be the end of The Worldwide Tour, but it would be the start of something else.

CHAPTER TWENTY-SEVEN

Date: April ?, 1962
Location: Alenuihaha Channel

The howling wind woke me. It whipped alongside the *Gracias* with a roar, pushing her sideways. Through the porthole I saw a flash of early sunlight and a sideways view of the water. It was early, yet the wind was high. I pushed myself out of the crevice I'd slid into between my bunk and the wall.

As I stepped onto the deck, my shaggy hair whipped back in the wind. It was blowing at least forty knots and the *Gracias* heeled port, leaning at a forty-five-degree angle. The rigging clanged and an eerie creaking came from the masts. I walked out carefully. My T-shirt caught the wind and twisted up my torso. I pulled it straight, only to let go and have it sail up again.

The sky was a flawless blue, clear but for a few clouds blown upward in long wisps. The wind made the sea around us rise and curl into tight, fast waves. One after another they spewed past, as if Neptune himself was spearing them on with his mighty trident. I watched them heaving by. What caused this on the open sea? There was no sign of a squall. Was a hurricane headed my way?

I turned around. There she lay, directly off the port bow. A long, wide mountain stretched the length of the coast. Her broad face caught the early sun coming from behind me. I saw a rocky rim along the top, and the ancient rain-washed gullies that spilled down her side. Near the bottom they spread into a wide field of black rocks that stretched to the sea. Silvery waves crashed into them, sending plumes of white water into the sky. I took in the view for an ecstatic moment, then went below to get my sextant. After taking a reading I consulted my charts. In the night we had blown into the Alenuihaha Channel. We were alongside the east end of the island of Maui, with the Big Island of Hawaii thirty miles to the east, making up the eastern edge of the channel. An asterisk at the bottom of the chart noted it was one of the roughest channels in the world.

The wail of the wind reminded me I needed to get back on deck and fix our direction. The *Gracias* stayed pitched at an angle, in perfect balance with the powerful gusts. Meanwhile, the waves were pushing us toward that rocky shore.

I raised the main and the foresail. They rustled loudly in the wind, and glowed white with the early morning sun. Setting the rudder to head starboard I went back to adjust the sails. We would be tacking into the wind; it was the only way to work our way through this gusty channel. But the *Gracias* wouldn't move forward. Instead, we lurched port, closer to the coast. Something was hanging us up. I looked aft. A line ran over the transom and dropped into the water. My sea anchor. Deployed any number of nights before, it still hung in the sea behind us, holding us there.

Sloppy and stupid of me. I hastened to the winch to pull it in.

I tried to ease starboard but the *Gracias* stayed facing straight ahead, lurched to the side, as waves continued to rush by. We were in irons; I had too much sail, it was capturing all the wind. We were being held in place, while slowly being pushed toward the rocks. Locking the tiller, I went to drop the foresail and reef the main. Once, twice, then three times. I quickly jumped back to the helm and eased her starboard. We were close hauled, on the edge of the "no go" zone, the place where the sails could no longer pick up any wind. It was the only position I could hold to get any movement. We began to go forward. The deck leveled a bit. We were heading north, through the channel toward Maui's north side and windward shores; I hoped from there it would be an easy sail to Honolulu. Maybe we would be there in time for supper.

But as the sun got higher, so did the winds. They were easily at fifty knots, maybe sixty. They whipped the very breath out of me. Going with only the triple-reefed main, we moved very slowly. My priority was only to keep the *Gracias* upright in this crazy storm of wind.

The water was incredible. We were heading into the wind-driven waves, and their peaks relentlessly washed over the bow. It was like trying to swim through a shore break that never ended. Curl after curl passed, leaving behind sprays of salty mist. I stayed at the helm and kept an eye on my sail. By my estimates, we were within ten degrees of disaster. If the wind banked a bit to the north the hull would heel further port and the waves crashing across deck would surely swamp us. I stayed where I was.

The morning passed. We crept along the coast, close enough that I could make out herds of cattle among the rocky pastures. I saw no people. There were no other boats.

Anyone who knew the waters here would surely stay out of this fetch of sea. We were closer to land than we had been in weeks, but struggling through the channel, an entire ocean seemed to stand in our way.

It was a battle of wills. The channel had her prerogative: for thousands of years she had captured the wind in this massive, thirty-mile-wide tunnel banked on each side by 10,000-foot volcanos, regardless of who chose to pass here and their intentions. She would do the same today. I had an objective of my own: to keep the *Gracias* and her crew above water. I hadn't come this far, finally in sight of land, to fail because of some wind. Damned if I was going to let this bloody channel doom me now.

I kept her close hulled. The *Gracias* was already pitched hard to her port side. There was less than a foot between the deck and the water. Foamy tops from the waves accumulated along the edge of the port bow like a snowbank. I didn't know how much further we had to go. I didn't want to be out here in the dark. Rough reefs trimmed this coastline. I couldn't navigate them in the dark and manage my sail. As the sun moved past its zenith, I adjusted my estimate to within five degrees of disaster.

A large black bird, a frigate of some sort, circled high above us. Using the very wind that I was fighting, it easily soared on the thermal drafts on its wide, sturdy wings. It made a big arc eastward, then dipped down and swooped across the bow of the *Gracias*. I saw the dark gray of its beak and a red pouch under its throat. Finding nothing of interest here, it lifted high again, flaunting its ease of flight in this impossible wind, then disappeared behind us. I didn't know if I should take it as an omen; was it a dark sign of death? Or a welcome to these islands?

I heard a hint of a jangle, then a swoosh, almost lost in the wind. An object was flying straight for my head. I ducked, and put up my left hand just in time to catch it. It was a pulley, swinging loose on its line. Over the course of the day, the strong winds had undone the knot that once held it fast. My hand stung from the impact of the sharp, heavy metal, hot from the sun. It surely would have knocked me out if it hit me in the forehead. My heart raced as I contemplated the pulley in my hand and saw the red swelling building in my palm. How close had I come to ending it all right here with a knock to the head? I looked up the mast to find the end of the line, hung up in the rigging; there was no way to right it now with my hands full at the helm and the *Gracias* pitching hard. I tossed the pulley in an under-hand pitch toward the mast, where it hit the deck, slid port, and dangled over the edge, its wheels playfully spinning in the mist of frothy water. I took a deep breath. I had to stay focused. I was using everything I had, and so far it was working. I had to stick with it.

I stood my watch, the only watch, legs bent and feet braced on the precariously slanted deck. My right hand was on the tiller, and my face was scoured by the wind and salt. I was exhausted. I hadn't eaten nor sat down all day. If it was the last thing I did on earth, we were going to clear the tip of the island and sail out of this miserable channel. While many things had gone amiss on this journey, I knew my fate was not to have it end here.

I sensed we were reaching the far northeast point of land as the wind began to come across the beam. The *Gracias* finally leveled as we turned west and came along the windward coast. With just the simple turn of the corner, the ocean calmed to a steady roll. It lay pale and silvery blue, reflecting the last of the day's sunlight off the pink fluffy clouds above. I barely noticed; I was scanning the water for a place to drop anchor. I found a small bay in the lee of a green valley wall, shallow but safe from the current.

With the wind calmed, I took a deep breath. The smell of land was overwhelming. I could discern the scent of every leaf on every plant. I could smell the rich soil and the bark on the trees. I longed to touch it all, to walk upon the grass in my bare feet. But I was beat. My shoulder ached, my palm felt swollen and stiff, and my legs trembled as I climbed below deck.

I ate my last can of chili sitting on the salon bench, spooning it straight from the can. I left it empty on the floor, the spoon tucked inside, and stretched out for a long nap.

I was surprised to wake from my deep sleep. I felt the presence of someone in the salon, a stranger observing me. I could feel his curiosity, wondering who I was and where I had come from. Yet when I opened my eyes I was alone.

I followed this strange feeling as I went on deck and looked ashore. Moonlight illuminated the narrow valley. Its walls were tall and steep and went back deep, hidden behind a thick forest of low leafy trees. I inhaled deeply, enjoying the fresh midnight air and the earthy smell. I watched the breeze ripple through the trees. There was a rustle in the tall grass along the shore. Was someone there? Was I imagining things?

I was exhausted beyond any point I'd experienced before. The stress of the trip had worn on my mind and body. Hadn't I seen my dad that time? Maybe my mind was deceiving me again. It was time to give up my curiosity and trust that all was as it should be. I needed to rest. In the morning I was hoping for a smooth sail to Honolulu. I would arrive in a real harbor, and be greeted by my fellow man. Comforted by that prospect, I eased down the companionway and into my cabin.

CHAPTER TWENTY-EIGHT

Date: April ?, 1962
Location: Honolulu Harbor

Every sailor knows first impressions in a new port can make or break you. The last thing I wanted to look like was a bedraggled castaway, even if that was how I was feeling. Navy training serves one well in preparing to look presentable for whomever you may encounter in your first steps on land.

I dropped anchor outside the breakwater and made ready with a refreshing swim, my first in several days. Next, I used one of my last remaining gallons of water and a sliver of soap to remove the salt. I was a deep tan all over, but for my rosy Scandinavian cheeks, now an even brighter red from yesterday's wind. My hair combed over easily, long and loose, but that was suitable, it was the style. However, there was no accounting for my beard. Having left it on its own for several weeks, my rusty razor was useless. I got out a pair of scissors and continued to work, peering into the tiny mirror in the head, turning my face at odd angles and adjusting it to and fro to see if things looked even. I quit before I was entirely satisfied, but so be it.

From the drawer beneath my bunk I pulled out my clean pair of dungarees, saved for the occasion.

I left the *Gracias* and took my skiff inside. Honolulu was a fair haven indeed, with its industrial piers, a string of warehouses, and cars parked along the wharf. It was reassuring; I saw strong evidence of the existence of my fellow man. A tall, square, concrete tower dominated the waterfront. Almost 200 feet tall, a large clock near its top told me it was just after ten o'clock. Above it, the stars and stripes waved hello. I was surprised to feel a flutter in my heart. Home, in a sense. Hawaii had joined the union a few years before.

It was quiet for midmorning. No tugs were out on the water, no longshoremen at work. I tied up easily and stepped ashore. Ah, the comfort of a concrete pier. I bent my legs, feeling the solid, still surface. My first steps were a little scraggly, like a crab moving side to side. But my land-legs came to me quickly as I was eager to find someone about. I followed the pier to the wharf.

"Ahoy, sailor!"

I turned around to see the man who would be my first friend in Honolulu. He had about three inches over my six-foot frame, and a linebacker's build. He was clean-shaven but for a mustache, and his black hair was trim on the sides and combed in a thick natural wave near the front. His brown eyes were keen, friendly, and full of mirth.

I had cleaned up pretty good on the *Gracias*, but the curious look on his face reminded me the standards of life ashore were different. My dungarees were wrinkled, my once-navy-blue shirt faded from being hung out over the rail to dry many times over. I still wasn't entire sure how my beard looked.

My joy at seeing another of my species quickly put any insecurities behind me. Instinctively, I gave him a salute, then held out my hand. He took it in his beefy one.

"Captain Ken Bohlin."

"Solomon Vaifale. You can call me Vai. You look like you've been away a piece. Where are you coming from, my brother?"

"A piece, absolutely. I believe I'm twenty-two days out of the Marquesas."

"The Marquesas?! Now's a strange time to come this way."

"It is. I was expecting fifteen to eighteen days at the most."

"What brings you to Honolulu?"

"I'm headed 'round the world. But when I lost my crew, I decided to come here for a respite, rather than make the long haul across the South Pacific."

"Ah, so I'm the lucky one to meet you, instead of my cousins in Samoa! How the fates have aligned! What came of your crew? I hope you didn't throw them over!" He laughed for a moment, but I saw the question in his eyes.

"I spared them that misfortune when I left them at Hiva Oa. Where can a man get a hot shower at this port? And maybe a cold beer?"

He smiled and looked into my face thoughtfully.

"You don't know what today is, Skipper?"

"By my guess it's about April 16th, maybe the 17th. I left the Marquesas about a week after the equinox. Am I right?"

"You've come a long piece for sure. It's April 22nd. Today is Easter Sunday."

My reckoning was off by five days. How did that happen? There were those lost hours, yes. Five days' worth? I was shocked. My navigating ability was appalling, and my pace atrocious. Twenty-seven days at sea. A shudder went through me and my feet seemed to grab hold of the ground in desperate relief we had made it at all. I shook my head. Easter? It couldn't be. I'd have to review my charts and plotting.

Vai clapped a hand on my shoulder.

"Don't worry about it, my friend, you're here now. I've got a place for you to get cleaned up. And a hot meal too. Let's go get you registered at the harbor master's. You have your paperwork with you? And you might want to send a telegram somewhere?"

"Yes, on both counts."

A lone man sat behind a desk in the telegram office. "Can I help you, son?"

I looked at my watch. It was 11:00 a.m. here; probably already dark on this spring evening back in Leicester. I pictured my family sitting around the kitchen table, digging into their plates filled with mashed potatoes and my mother's special honey-baked ham. Claude Vanderwolf, the postman and telegram operator, would likely also be enjoying Easter dinner with his family. But, I reasoned, if he's already deep in a bottle of scotch he'd probably send his son Hank on his bike to deliver my message. My mother would ask him to stay for dessert. Hank wouldn't mind.

I had the operator tap out: "Arrived Hon. HI today. All well. Happy Easter."

Vai was as good as his word. He said on any other day he would have taken me home with him, but his family was busy with Easter celebrations. "You won't find any beer there either!" he laughed. As we rode in his battered Datsun truck he asked where I was from, my nationality, and about my maritime background. We went a short way along the coast and past a tree-filled park lining the beach. Vai turned off into a parking lot. We were at a small marina. Not far away was the prominent shape of Diamond Head Mountain. I had seen her before, on postcards and in shipping magazines. She sat overlooking the famous pearly white strand of beach. I could hardly believe I was here, taking in this view in person.

"Welcome to the Ala Wai Yacht Harbor! You'll probably want to move your boat here later," Vai said. "They usually keep a few berths open for visitors."

We walked over to a square, gray concrete building with an emblem above the door proclaiming it the "Hawaii Yacht Club." Inside, Vai introduced me at the front desk as a guest of Captain Lyman. Why wasn't I a guest of his? The name—lie-man—maybe it was a funny ruse? As I was at his mercy, I said nothing and followed him in.

Vai led me through the lobby and into the lounge, where several bamboo-trimmed sofas were arranging in neat sitting areas. Looking through a huge picture-glass window ahead of us was the marina itself. There was an assortment of boats there, many which outshone the *Gracias* in size and flash. A pair of gentlemen came to stand alongside us as we looked.

Vai turned to greet them. "Ah, Captain Lyman! Happy Easter!" He held out his hand, and while shaking, pulled the man to him for a hug and clap on the shoulder. "How are you, my friend?"

"Just fine, Vai, just fine. Happy Easter to you too. I'm surprised to find you down here frolicking around the waterfront today. What brings you by?" Captain Lyman already had his curious eyes trained on me.

"Captain, I'd like you to meet Captain Bohlin, a Kings Point man."

We shook hands. "Call me Ken," I clarified. He looked a few years my senior, and had sandy-brown hair swept over the top of his head. He gave a big smile under his thick handlebar mustache. "David. And this is my associate Captain Campbell, Bob."

Campbell was older than the two of us, with salt-and-pepper hair and a portly build. He lifted his chin toward me. "You look like you've just come off the water, Captain!"

"Is it that plain? Well, yes, I just came across from the Marquesas, single-handed. Twenty-seven days, I'm told. Arrived this morning."

"This morning! Twenty-seven days! 'You're told!'" Lyman exclaimed. "No wonder you've got a salty look about you. I'll bet you've got some tales to tell!" He stood with both hands deep in the front pockets of his pants, jingling the change there, looking at me squarely. "You, my friend, have just joined a very elite club. Not many make that crossing solo."

I hadn't thought about it that way. "I guess you might be right."

"I know I am! What are you sailing?"

"My forty-foot schooner, the *Gracias*, out of Annapolis."

"Single-handed on a schooner? How'd you fix your rigging?" Before I answered he interrupted with a wave of his hand.

"Never mind that for now, there will be lots of time to hear all the details. Why don't you visit the locker room and get cleaned up? We'll get you signed in as my guest. They're putting on a big Easter meal in the dining room later. Care to join us? At least for a beer?"

"I believe I will. Thank you, Captain."

Vai gave me a wink and said to Captain Lyman, "Already taken care of. I'll show him to the head."

"Sounds good, Vai. Enjoy your Easter." He gave Vai a hug and looking over his shoulder toward me he called out, "Meet us upstairs in the bar!"

That first shower ashore after twenty-seven days was wonderful. The shower was tiled in clean white ceramic squares, and it soon filled with steam. I found a bottle of shampoo on the rack and washed my hair three times. I lathered up with the thick bar of Ivory soap, and let the bubble stay on my skin, enjoying their warm, soapy smell. After some time the heat faded a bit; had I emptied the hot-water tank? In short order I rinsed and stepped out into the locker room, thick white towel wrapped around my slim waist.

Vai was standing across the room at the counter, trying to examine his hair in the steamed-up mirror.

"Ah, I bet you're feeling better!"

"Like a million bucks!"

"That's great, my friend. Look, I have to get going, but I thought you might want to make use of these."

In one hand he held a razor—I laughed. In the other he held a hanger with a clean, pressed shirt. Arranged across a faint tan background were blue flowers and what looked like sails, and maybe a bird or two. A black zigzag-like pattern was printed here and there across the fabric. It was vivid and bold, and looked very tropical. I had never seen anything like it. He held it out to me with pride.

"I think this Aloha shirt will fit you. It's one of my good ones, I keep it here for those 'just in case' days. I think today's one of those. Leave it here when you're *pau*"—he knocked on one of the metal lockers—"and I'll get it washed for the next time."

"Thank you, Vai, I really appreciate it."

"No problem, my friend." He gave me another big smile. "I think you're going to fit in just fine around here."

"Thanks." Now I awkwardly held the razor in one hand and the hanger in the other; I put the razor down on the counter and held out my hand. "Thanks for all you've done. It won't be forgotten."

"I know, Captain Ken, I know it. And one of these days, I want to hear all your stories at sea. I know you must have a few!" He turned to leave, calling out "*A hui hou!*" over his shoulder as he went.

I climbed the outdoor staircase and stopped at the top to look around. Ahead of me was the marina; onshore behind me a range of deep green mountains were nestled together, disappearing into gray rain clouds above. Hawaii was more beautiful than I'd imagined. I wished BJ were here to see this. Yet if he had continued on we might be in Samoa by now. Arriving in Honolulu was a fate that was solely my own.

I looked again at the grand expanse of the Pacific Ocean, appearing calm and innocent in the bright, clear noon. I had just come across this great prairie of sea and still I was only beginning to fathom her size, her depth, and her might. Tacking through the channel yesterday I fought against her wind; in the squalls I had captured it. Whichever direction it blew, I worked my sails to keep moving, to stay afloat. Without any real plan I used the wind, the sea, the tools I had at hand and my own wit to make it across. Four thousand miles. I supposed Lyman was right; I was now in a unique class, one I had never intended to be part of. I had made the crossing solo. All the things I thought I could plan against, everything I thought wouldn't happen to me, had happened anyway. The frustration on the doldrums days; getting lost chasing the wind; the confusion and the loneliness. My mind had been badly befuddled. My reckoning was off by five days. I still couldn't believe it. In the end, I wasn't any better than the best of them. It took me down a notch.

But I had made it. And I could count myself among a new brotherhood; only those who've been there can understand what it's like. I had just completed an unplanned solo crossing of 4,000 miles. After that, anything was possible.

"Ah, there he is, a new man!" The satisfying scent of baking ham filled my nostrils as I stepped into the building. Lyman and Campbell were sitting with arms resting on a thick wooden bar. Overhead hung triangular flags representing nations around the world. Around the corner from the bar I saw the dining room, featuring another great picture window that looked out over the marina and sea beyond.

"How are you, Captain Ken?"

"Great, Captain Lyman, thank you for your hospitality. I sure feel better."

"How about a cold one, to make it a real winner? Or something stronger, if you'd like?"

They both had frosty half-full mugs before them. "A beer would be terrific. Thank you."

Lyman gave a wave at the bartender, indicating one more.

"So, Campbell and I have been making a wager here. He thinks you put your crew overboard, somewhere in the high seas." He gave a wink in Campbell's direction. "Me, I have a good instinct for men. You have to, with the business we're in. And I don't see you as the killing type. Of course, anything can happen out there. The fury that comes out of men never ceases to amaze me." He gave me another once-over, playful now. "I don't see you that way;

but something must have happened. Not many undertake a solo crossing on a whim. Now that you're here, why don't you enlighten us? We can't wait to hear the whole story."

The bartender set a thick mug of beer before me. I took a long sip, and wiped the froth off my lips with the back of my hand. How wonderful it felt. To be ashore, sitting on a steady barstool that didn't rock or heave. To taste the sweet tang of ice-cold beer in my mouth. To know Easter dinner was around the corner. To know I had made it, the *Gracias* and I had arrived, safe and sound. Twenty-seven days alone at sea. And here I sat, among my kind, with new friends eager to hear my story.

"Well, gentlemen, let me tell you. Things were going along swell, until the broad fell overboard."

AUTHOR'S NOTE

Left at Hiva Oa is based on a true story.

The *Gracias* continued to be home for Captain Ken for the next few years as he lived on board at the Ala Wai Yacht Harbor. This is where he met my mother, on a blind date.

They married in Singapore in October 1966. Captain Ken was working on a contract assignment as a tugboat captain in Vietnam. He was there for two back-to-back nine-month contracts and returned to Honolulu in 1967.

He went on to become first mate of the *M.V. Hawaiian Princess*, an interisland cargo carrier. His route took him through the island chain on a weekly rotation. I was born in Honolulu in 1971; my brother in 1973. As Oahu became more industrialized my parents decided to move to one of the more rural neighbor islands. We moved to Maui and lived in a small rented house in Waihee Valley. Later they built a house in the Haiku countryside, where I spent the rest of my childhood.

Having learned to navigate all of the island ports on the *Hawaiian Princess*, Captain Ken became certified as a state harbor pilot, and was hired on as Pilot #7, the harbor pilot for the port of Kahului. As he said, "it's an ideal job for any seaman who also wants to keep a garden." In this role, he captained every ship that came into Kahului Harbor. He would ride out past the breakwater on the pilot boat, skippered by Captain Bill Clark, to meet incoming ships. Once abreast, the ship's crew threw a long ladder over the rail. He made a quick leap to catch it as the pilot boat crested on the current, then climbed up to the deck, where he was escorted to the main deck. Here he assumed command, taking all means of ships through the breakwater of Kahului Harbor, dodging the tricky winds that could come about and safely docking the ship. He handled fishing boats from Japan, "tin plate" ships bringing metal for the pineapple cannery, cruise ships, military and cargo ships from around the world. He delighted in the variety of ships and the people he met on board. A true sailor at heart, everyone he met was a new friend and he happily greeted them upon their arrival to Maui.

His days on the high seas were over. He would never sail across the Pacific again.

I asked him once if he regretted never completing his journey around the world. I was back from college, tagging around after him in the garage, his favorite place to do woodworking and to contemplate. He was heavier now, with the same lean frame but also a round protruding belly, the result of the medications since his kidney transplant. He sat in the breezeway, on a stool he'd made with four simple spindle legs and a square plywood plank nailed on top. For finishing touches, he had rounded the corners of the seat and painted the whole thing tractor green. Old Hawaiian songs played from a small transistor radio on a shelf above his workbench. Neither of us knew he was in his last years of life; side effects from his kidney disease were wearing on his body and would cause his death just days after my college graduation.

His answer that day gives me comfort still.

He looked out across the green sloping yard, past the plumeria and macadamia nut trees, beyond the verdant pastures to the ocean that lay there, a bold blue strip that filled half the horizon and met with a brilliant sky. "Sometimes I do," he admitted, nodding his head. He held his gaze over all that green and blue. "But things turned out pretty good this way too."

Thanks, Dad.

ACKNOWLEDGEMENTS

Many people from many parts of my life helped in some aspect of writing *Left at Hiva Oa*. I am grateful for their help, and more so, for the relationships that made it possible.

My deepest gratitude to:

My mother, Jennifer Bohlin, for always supporting me, no matter what wild idea I bring to her; for holding on to that box of dad's old stuff; and for exchanging Christmas cards with Jean for over 45 years.

Jean Robeson, for sharing her memories of the journey and warmly encouraging my work.

Mike and Margie Durant, for sharing the story about the cigarettes, and for introducing my parents all those years ago.

Dave and Annewim Brown, for introducing me to your neighbor, who shared many great "at sea" stories with me.

My many early readers, for your valuable input, enthusiasm and encouragement.

Cindy and Fred Rampey, for letting me "drive" the *Sol Mate*, and experience what it's like to be at the helm.

Virgie, Kalei and Kristin for making my first writer's group such a positive experience; and Jasmyne Boswell for your leadership and brilliant advice.

Cat Sides for getting me jump-started with NaNoWriMo, your many suggestions for resources, and guiding me through the process.

Danielle Corriveau, for your words of encouragement, which came back to me time after time.

Marissa Bholan and the staff at the USMMA Alumni Association & Foundation, Inc.

Capt. Ed Enos, of the Hawaii Pilots Association, and the family of Capt. David Lyman.

Lourdes Venard, for your excellent feedback and suggestions.

Paul, for asking me about this project every Thursday.

My #badass lady friends.

ECHO, know it or not, you were with me all along.

Pamela Newsom, for your friendship all these years.

Byron Tabisola, for your consistent, absolute support.

BIBLIOGRAPHY

Department of Health, Education, and Welfare, *The Ship's Medicine Chest and First Aid at Sea*. Washington, DC: United States Government Printing Office, 1955

Dubach, Harold W. and Taber, Robert W. *Questions About the Oceans*. Washington, D.C.: U.S. Naval Oceanographic Office, 1968

Graham, Robin Lee. *Dove*. New York: Harper & Row, 1972

Hiscock, Eric. *Voyaging Under Sail*. London: Oxford University Press, 1959

Jarman, Colin. *The Essential Knot Book*. Camden, Maine: International Marine Publishing Company, 1984

Marsh, George. *Flash the Lead Dog*. New York: Grosset & Dunlap, 1927

Pukui, Mary Kawena, *ʻŌlelo Noʻeau Hawaiian Proverbs & Poetic Sayings*. Honolulu: Bishop Museum Press, 1983

Slocum, Joshua. *Sailing Alone Around the World.* New York: The Century Co., 1899

Thompson, Nainoa, *Predicting Weather: Reading Clouds and Sea States. Hōkūleʻa* website: 2000

Midships 1957. Kings Point U.S. Merchant Marine Academy, 1957

Wikipedia, *Glossary of Nautical Terms*

ABOUT THE AUTHOR

Malia Bohlin was born and raised in Hawaii. She attended the University of Colorado in Boulder, earning a Bachelor of Science in Journalism and Mass Communication, and later received her Master's Degree in Non-Profit Management from Regis University in Denver. She works in fundraising and as a PATH International certified instructor in a therapeutic horseback riding program. Ms. Bohlin loves to travel, read, ride, write, and sometimes run half-marathons. *Left at Hiva Oa* is her first novel. Learn more at www.maliabohlin.com

Made in the USA
San Bernardino, CA
13 January 2018